SURVIVING YOUR WORST NIGHTMARE

A GUIDE FOR THE BETRAYED

Patti Snodgrass

Scripture taken from THE MESSAGE. Copyright © by Eugene H. Peterson, 1993, 1994,1995,1996. Used by permission of NavPress Publishing Group.

Scripture taken from the New Century Version ®. Copyright © 2005 by Thomas Nelson, Inc. Used by permission. All rights reserved.

Scripture taken from the Contemporary English Version © 1991, 1992, 1995 by American Bible Society, Used by Permission.

Scripture quotations marked NLT are taken from the Holy Bible, New Living Translation, copyright 1996, 2004. Used by permission of Tyndale House Publishers, Inc., Wheaton, Illinois 60189. All rights reserve

Grateful acknowledgment is made to HEY Design for the cover art direction, lay out and design. Used by permission. All rights reserved worldwide.

ISBN: 1456334077
ISBN-13: 9781456334079
Library of Congress Control Number: 2010916794

To my Guide,
I will never forget

CONTENTS

What Readers Are Saying...vii

Before You Begin.. xi

PART I A Nightmare In the Heart..................................... xvii

So It Begins..xix

1 Why?..................................... 1

2 The Wilderness Ahead................................. 13

3 How Did I Get Here?................................. 23

4 My Reality.. 41

5 Don't Open That Door.............................. 65

6 Behind Closed Doors.............................. 79

7 Love Forsaken 97

PART II Survival Guide—Chronicles of a Wounded
Heart.. 109

8 Find True North................................... 111

9 Have a Plan.................................. 131

10 Endurance 153

11 Discern the Situation—Trust Your Instincts........ 171

12 Consider the Risks.............................. 183

13 Look for a Clearing............................201

14 Take Hold of Courage...........................225

15 Never Give Up................................ 245

PART III The Awakening 263

16 North 265

A Special Thank You 275

WHAT READERS ARE SAYING

I read *Surviving Your Worst Nightmare: A Guide For the Betrayed* shortly after discovering that my husband had betrayed our wedding vows. It was comforting to know that someone had experienced what I was going through, and that I, too, could survive. It was reassuring to hear that my crazy thinking and roller coaster emotions were normal. It was also helpful to learn that the desires I had—to stay with my husband and work on our marriage—were not foolish. *Surviving Your Worst Nightmare: A Guide for the Betrayed* is not a one-time read; I often referred back to the book as I tried to live my new life after broken wedding vows. I found that Patti's recommended practice of "Face it, Embrace it, Mourn it, and Move on" has been especially helpful in the healing process, not only as my husband and I worked on restoring our marriage, but also with other past relational hurts in my life. I have found hope again for my future. I would highly recommend this book to anyone who has been betrayed by a spouse or loved one, whether it was yesterday, or years ago.

—*Ann Roth, A survivor*

If you want the truth about the devastating effects of adultery upon a spouse, and how to navigate gracefully through that pain, you have stumbled on the right book.

With gut-wrenching honesty, Patti Snodgrass shares the "real state of affairs". Someone once told me "Truth without grace is just plain mean." No need to worry about that here. This is a book full of grace and truth.

—*Dave Browning, Lead Pastor, Christ the King Community Church, and author of Deliberate Simplicity*

Whether you are trying to survive the aftermath of your spouse's unfaithfulness, or you have been the unfaithful one, this book is for you. Having been on both sides of betrayal—being a betrayer, and having been betrayed—I know the pain and heartbreak that an affair creates. Patti's survival story is honest, informative and insightful. The guide section will help you process the emotional trauma that the affair has brought into your life. A must read, not only for the faithful, but for the unfaithful as well.

—*Lily Conant*

Since it rings true that, "all humans are born broken, spend their lives mending, and the grace of God is the glue," *Surviving Your Worst Nightmare: A Guide for the Betrayed* is a lifeline for all of us. For many, however, the universal brokenness Eugene O'Neil described is intensified by early traumatizing life experiences. Patti awakened to a nightmare in her marriage, and though paralyzed, realized the nightmare was rooted in her early tragic childhood. I salute Patti's decision to face her early tragedies so she could be a healthy human being. Early on, she resolved to share her story because it just might "connect" with someone who is trapped and sees no "way out." Patti's magnetic story line and her gentle care for readers are proofs that she writes with mellow authority and wisdom, which forms only in the crucible of suffering and grief. Patti's wisdom is easily accessible. She is eager to walk with anyone who meets a "nightmare" horror.

—*Donald M. Joy, Ph. D., Professor of Human Development and Family Studies, Asbury Theological Seminary, Wilmore, Kentucky*

Before You Begin

If this book is in your hands, your spouse has most likely betrayed you; your worst nightmare has just robbed you of the life that you desired for yourself. This catastrophic event of infidelity has altered your life forever. I wrote this guidebook using my own real life experience of how I survived my husband's unfaithfulness. It is my hope that my story will help you navigate through the nightmare that has violently shattered your world.

As I began writing this guidebook, one of my mentors gave me a piece of advice. She suggested that I tell a portion of my whole story, from my earliest memories to the present tragedy, in order for you to truly know me. She felt that I needed to become personally vulnerable for my readers. With much reflection, I took her advice.

My goal in sharing small vignettes of my life, before and after my worst nightmare tainted my dreams, is to let you know that I am a normal person, with issues and brokenness that hindered finding my way through the unfamiliar wilderness of my husband's unfaithfulness. I stumbled, I fell, and I continually picked myself up—over and over again. The reason I was able to heal from this trauma was because I was determined to get beyond the excruciating heart pain; no matter how long it would take, or how difficult it was, I wanted to heal. I have found that it is possible to live the life that I had always dreamed even when the journey through betrayal to healing seemed devastatingly hopeless.

As we begin this journey together, I recommend that you be diligent in your search for a competent counselor. If this seems overwhelming, I have put together a list of qualifying questions in the Appendix to help you interview and find a skilled therapist. When you find the right therapist you will be richly rewarded. I also recommend that you purchase a large spiral notebook and a favorite pen. I believe having an experienced counselor, and journaling are two of the most important first steps in order to begin your healing journey.

You will be helped by this guidebook, even if you feel that journaling is "not your thing." Many to whom I have spoken struggle with journaling, but I believe that this is a very important exercise in your journey towards survival. If you are one who believes that you are not a writer and would have difficulty journaling, I encourage you to give it a try. I have found that there is a distinct difference between the ones who survive their nightmares with journaling and those who do not. It seems that those who write process their pain more rapidly and with more clarity than those who decide that writing is too difficult. If you choose to write, scattered throughout the guide there are questions or thoughts that will help you reflect and process your feelings. These times of reflection along your reading journey will prove vital for your healing; I cannot emphasize this enough.

As you read this guidebook, a memory or a feeling may burst forth because we share the same emotional experience. You may find that something I've shared triggers a thought or feeling; this is the best time to document these thoughts. An unearthed emotion that erupts is important information; it can aid you as your heart and mind begin to heal from this betrayal. I call this practice listening with the heart.

Minutes after my husband's confession, in my despair, I called my counselor. I wanted her to tell me what to do, but she would not. Instead, she quietly said, "Follow your heart; you will then make the right decision."

Following my counselor's advice would prove to be extremely difficult for me. I would second-guess every thought and action. At times I felt vulnerable, confused, and frightened as I tried to listen to the counsel of my heart. "What if I make the wrong decision?" Learning to distinguish what my head was screaming and what my heart was trying to tell me would become one of the most challenging phases as I tried to survive this nightmare.

For my healing journey to begin I had to step out onto this new path of listening with my heart and develop the ability to trust myself. This was quite daunting. I had to learn to be okay with being alone at times and not sur-rounding myself with well-meaning friends and family. Our loved ones care so deeply for us and, because of their strong convictions and concerns for us, they often do not offer the best advice for our life. Because of their own need to support and protect us, and their own need to help themselves cope with our painful situation, they may with good intentions speak out of their sympathy, often missing what we need. They may try to persuade your head to think one way or another, but your heart is your own. I had to learn to be okay with being alone with myself, alone with my heart.

I know for some of you, your present nightmare may be the worst event that ever happened to you. You may have been completely knocked off course and are stumbling among the shattered remnants of your forsaken love. I also know the healing process will be difficult and at many stages along the way you may want to give up. The work will feel too intense and emotionally draining or the financial strain will seem too burdensome. I urge you to persevere.

I hope my story of survival is an encouragement to you as you navigate through your own story of betrayal that has destroyed the dreams of the life that you had. My desire for you, as you walk with me through my background stories and as you begin your own story of listening with your heart, is that you will find comfort in knowing you are not alone on this journey, that you may find hope rising and that you may soon believe you can survive your worst nightmare.

*A story is a way to say something
that can't be said any other way, and it takes every
word in the story to say what the meaning is.
You tell a story because a statement would be inadequate.*

Flannery O'Conner

Now for some heart work.

Rainer Maria Rilke

PART I

A Nightmare In the Heart

During his sleep, his soul was oppressed
with a "thick and dreadful darkness," which seemed to
smother him and felt like a nightmare in his heart ...

F. B. Meyer

Introduction
So It Begins...

August 3, 2001

I had walked quite a distance from our cabin. My subconscious mind alerted me that something was not quite right. In that moment my meditative thoughts collided with the actual desperation of my situation.

What had I heard? What caused an icy chill to course through my body? I heard it again, farther away this time. It sounded like someone screaming. I glanced around. Everything seemed fine until, in the distance, I saw them running. Couples who had been in a romantic interlude with one another were now racing for their cabins with terror on their faces. The families that had been out enjoying the countryside were now running as fast as they could, carrying their traumatized children in a frantic attempt to escape. I was completely aware of the screaming people running and stumbling past me, looks of horror on their faces. Some were badly cut and bleeding. But I felt like I was in a trance, as though some magnetic spell held me captive. I could not turn and run. Instead, I seemed inexplicably drawn toward whatever they were fleeing.

Moments before, I had been lured outside into the crisp, fresh mountain air to capture the pleasant fragrance of morning. Now, the stench of fear and blood completely awakened my senses. I was now a hostage to the terrorizing scene playing out before me.

One Hour Earlier

The morning began for me before the sun rose. I started wrestling with the daily 'to do's' that rob you of the last precious moments of morning sleep. You know, those days when your mind kicks in before your body. I was anticipating that the day ahead would be a pleasant one.

The family was all sleeping cozily throughout the rustic log cabin that we had rented for the long weekend reunion. The sound of my father's deep throaty snores echoed throughout the lodge. Thank goodness my husband and I had the room farthest from his. The kids can sleep through anything, credit due to our early childhood training of vacuuming under their cribs while they were napping. My brothers and their wives still snuggled in their warm beds, enjoying the plump down comforters that make you want to linger longer and enjoy those last minutes of comfort from a good night's rest.

The lasting scent of the cedar log that had burned all night in the river rock fireplace filled the main living area of the beautiful log cabin. What a delightful morning. I decided that I would crawl out from under my comfy covers, slip downstairs and surprise the family with a hearty homemade breakfast. Dark roasted European coffee, fresh squeezed orange juice and fluffy pancakes smothered in delicious maple syrup ought to do the trick. I thought that I would also fry up some seasoned homemade sausage that I had purchased at the local market on our way up to this mountain retreat. This was going to be quite an accomplishment for me, since I do not particularly enjoy cooking. But the thought of the tantalizing aromas of brewed coffee and of sizzling sausage arousing the senses of each slumbering person made my heart happy. Those enticing comfort food scents can cause even the most dreadful "not a morning person" to wake up with a smile on his or her face.

Coffee was first on the list. The grinder hummed as I ground the beans, filling the air with a pleasing aroma. My mouth began to salivate just anticipating my first taste of the dark brew.

The kitchen was enormous. If I were a chef it would be a dream kitchen. The stove was one of those fancy "it can do everything for you" models. I thought to myself, *"Okay, I can cook on this mama!"* The oversized appliance was a bit intimidating, but I was willing to give it a try.

I began mixing the batter for the pancakes and paused after a few stirs, lifting a large, steaming coffee mug to my lips. I looked out in amazement through the large windows that covered the entire front of the cabin. The sun was just beginning to swell over the eastern hillside, casting a golden glow on the western mountain slope. It took my breath away. The early morning mist was slowly rising, giving the scene an eerie appearance. Smoke from the chimneys of all the occupied cabins was hovering in magical displays throughout the canyon. Dew was glistening on the tall grasses. The mountain chickadees were already busy visiting the many bird feeders lined along the back deck. I was in awe at the beauty that surrounded me on all sides.

My mind started to wander. What a stunning world God created! How sad that, most of the time, we are too busy in our daily lives to really stop and take notice. I guess that is why we need to get away to these mountain retreats and slow down enough to let the Creator show us His handiwork. "Well, God, I noticed." I planned to savor every moment of this weekend and soak in all aspects of His incredible creation.

The batter was at the right consistency, just enough lumps and bubbles, and the sausage was already sizzling on the grill. I had by now attempted a few of those first pancakes to see if the grill was hot enough and began to panic. The sausage was going to take longer to cook than I thought. The pancakes were starting to pile up.

I could hear sounds of stretching and yawning upstairs in the loft; down the hallway the shower was running. My plan had worked. My sleeping family was waking up for the first day of our weekend get-together.

I have not yet mastered the skill of getting all the food ready at the same time—you know, the kind of skill that, no matter what's cooking, the food comes out hot and perfect. Nor would I any time soon. As I struggled with my "timing issues," my husband joined me in the kitchen and began to criticize my inability to get all the food on the table, fully cooked and timed just right. He took the spatula out of my hand and said, "I'll do it!" in a demeaning voice. On any other day I would have reacted differently. But today, I was not going to respond and get myself all worked up and start my weekend in a negative mood. I had had many experiences in my marriage where I "didn't do things right," according to my husband. Many of the difficulties in our twenty-one years of marriage seemed to be "*my fault*," and the comments that were made over those long years that "*I needed to see a counselor and work on my issues*" were lodged in my mind. So of course I knew it was my fault that breakfast was now going to be ruined. Nobody likes cold pancakes, well, except our dogs Maggie and Jake.

Knowing that the breakfast preparation was now in skilled hands, I decided to pour myself another cup of coffee, add my favorite flavored creamer and take a quick walk outside to breathe in some fresh mountain air. I put on my sage green fleece jacket, zipped it up to my chin, stepped outside and allowed this mountain retreat to take me captive by its wonderful gift of beauty and tranquility.

There is nothing like the scent of the early morning air; there is an aura of sweetness to it. The combination of pine and aspen trees, wet grass, morning dew and the chill in the air makes for an intoxicating experience. It was so stimulating that I felt an urge to walk down the long winding path. As I strolled, immersed in the incredible sights and smells of this amazing place, I noticed that I was not the only one who had the idea of coffee and a walk. Many other occupants of this little community were enjoying a quiet, peaceful, leisurely stroll as well.

As I continued on down the rocky path I took my time, soaking in the splendor of this alluring mountain sanctuary. I sensed I was being drawn to something, I wasn't sure what, but it felt as if I didn't have a choice. I continued to walk slowly, carefully sipping my steaming beverage.

I could see that the area around me was surrounded by ranch land. Off in the distance I noticed cattle grazing and the sound of calves bawling as the mother cows were searching for their young to feed them. As I continued to stroll, I pondered on how nature takes care of itself. Mothers always want to nurture their offspring. I love how God designed that.

I observed that there were now many people out and about. Couples arm in arm or holding hands, looking dreamily into each other's eyes, talking non-stop or giggling at something that was said. For a moment I started to get caught up in the fantasy of my husband and me with an incredible relationship where I felt safe and secure, where I knew that he loved me because of the way he honored and cherished me, like he said he would on our wedding day. I am not sure how long I had been engrossed in this fantasy when piercing screams startled my thoughts back to reality.

Some of the people running past me had what looked like huge gaping wounds. One man was lying on the gravel road with his bloody face buried into the chest of what looked at first glance like a woman. Because they were so badly injured and bleeding, I was not certain exactly what gender they were. This tranquil place had suddenly become a scene of violence and chaos.

For a moment I stopped and looked around at my surroundings. When I left my cabin to begin my morning stroll, I had noticed the cattle that were grazing in the pastures on my right and on my left. At closer examination, what I had perceived before to be cows were actually enormous black bears. There were hundreds of them, and they were attacking the guests of this mountain refuge. I couldn't believe the scene that was unfolding right before my eyes. I stood frozen, unable to move.

There is no way to describe the brutality that I was witnessing; the screams still haunt me even to this day. Every direction I turned the sounds of bones crushing and flesh tearing surrounded me. Deafening cries of death and pain echoed in my head. I could not escape the viciousness of evil that was all around me. I felt a wave of nausea coming up the back of my throat; the bile was burning my esophagus, causing me to try to clear my throat but to no avail. The stench of all the slaughter and carnage was becoming too difficult for me to manage. I felt as if I were going to collapse, but my survival instinct bolted through my adrenal glands and I knew I had to get myself away from this horrifying situation.

The sudden rush of adrenaline caused me to spin quickly to my left and with great speed and agility I jumped over the grey, weathered split rail fence that lined the gravel road. With increasing difficulty I ran as fast as I could through the overgrown field, jumping over the deep furrows and dodging the many boulders that dotted the ground. From behind I could hear the terrifying sounds of a bear charging me. Somewhere in the back of my mind I remembered that one was not supposed to try to outrun a bear. Extremely fatigued, I stopped dead in my tracks.

In the midst of an impending attack, just like in the movies, everything slows down and the sounds around you become muffled. It is really like that; everything is silent, in an unnatural kind of way. In the pandemonium of this horrific event I knew there was no conceivable way to avoid the imminent violence, so I stood still waiting for the assault, surrendering to a quick death. I knew by what I had witnessed over the last several minutes that the pain of the attack would be severe. I stood motionless, silent. Just seconds before, I had heard the thundering charge of a giant bear crashing over the fence, but now there was absolute silence, except for the deep inhaling and exhaling of my own breath.

I waited for what seemed a lifetime—still no attack. The silence was piercing, intense. I gathered as much courage as I could muster and slowly turned my head toward the road to see why I was not being charged. I could not believe what I was witnessing. The vicious creature had stopped dead in its tracks just a few feet from me and was now motionless, staring lifelessly to my right as if it had no power on its own to finish what it had started to do: kill me.

Slowly, fearfully, I followed its stare, holding my breath so as not to make any sound that would startle the black beast from its trance-like state. I cautiously turned to see what had halted the attack and gasped at what I saw. Just to my right, standing more than twelve feet tall was the most repulsive creature I had ever seen. Its body was covered in knotted, mangled hair; the vile odor of its breath was sickening. As the beast growled through its blood stained fangs, flesh and saliva came spewing out. Its eyes glared down at me, piercing my soul with deadly hatred and contempt. It was in that moment that I realized I was not standing face to face with a creature from this world. I was standing face to face with Satan himself. The Prince of Darkness, the one who seeks to devour and destroy, was only a few feet from me.

There was no time to move. The first strike was excruciating, brutal. The claws that struck me were long, razor-sharp and soiled with a previous victim's blood. One swift hit and its gruesome nails sliced through my flesh. The force was so unbelievable that it nearly knocked me to the ground. Regaining my posture and reeling in pain from the wound that had just been inflicted on me, I was going into shock. I could not comprehend what was happening. Numbed by the violence I forced myself to gaze upon the long, jagged opening that now covered the left side of my chest. With robotic motion I placed both hands on the deep gash, thinking that I might stop the gushing blood. With every heart-pumping beat I felt my life draining away. I thought to myself, "*So this is it; this is how it ends.*" Then without pause, the gruesome beast raised its monstrous claws a second time to administer the final blow and as he did, the merciless evil creature spoke in the most terrifying spine-chilling voice, "*I AM GOING TO DESTROY YOUR LIFE!*"

As the beast's heavy claws came crashing down, incredible courage and strength came over me. It was as if some supernatural force took over all functions of my body. I was determined to fight, and even more determined to live. I was not ready to die; I would fight with everything I had in me. Just seconds before the mortal blow finished the task, I seized the beast's grotesque paws with both of my blood-stained hands and I screamed with such rage, such passion, "*NO, YOU WON'T!*" and I shoved the beast away.

I will never forget the look in its eyes, as this hideous creature stood there confounded. The fiery contempt that had been in his eyes just seconds before, was now gone. He had been defeated; confused, he turned swiftly and fled.

Sudden Awakening

Had this wide-awake nightmare been a premonition? Soon enough, I would discover that unfolding events following this mid-summer night's dream would alter my life forever.

Later that week I had an appointment with my counselor and I shared my dream with her. Her response, "You are under an attack of some sort!"

We talked a little more about its meaning and then moved on to the real reason for my scheduled time. My marriage was in a tumultuous downward spiral of unresolved issues. I was having great difficulty understanding my husband's perplexing behaviors and my responses to them. At times I literally thought that my head would explode. I thought that I must be the sickest person in the world. You know the hamster in the exercise wheel syndrome, the same old arguments about the same old issues and never any resolution? This was my marriage.

At the same time that I was dealing with the emotional strain of my disappointing and dysfunctional marriage, my three sons were creating unbelievable havoc in their lives by their irresponsible choices. I obviously was having difficulty raising socially and academically responsible boys as well as being a very messed up wife.

Was this my life? Was I condemned to live a life of unfulfilled dreams and failures?

The old adage "When it rains, it pours," described my life perfectly. As these daily trials continually pummeled me, my counselor had begun to unravel the tangled mess of my wounded childhood that for so long had been affecting the way I responded to all of the conflicts in my life. The revelations of my past and the emotional roller coaster ride of the present would accompany me much of the time and cause me to become extremely emotionally fatigued. I wondered at times how I would ever survive my life of constant confusion, discontentment and chaos.

And then, what had been foretold came to pass. One year, two months and three days after that terrorizing August nightmare, my world and my life as I knew it *was* completely destroyed.

> *Journal Entry, October 6, 2002*
> *Today my life is over.*
> *Today my husband confessed of being unfaithful*
>   *to me.*
> *Twenty-three years ago on this day my husband*
>   *told me that he loved me for the very first time.*
> *Today he told me that he never really loved me.*
> *What is real in my life?*
> *What is happening to me?*

When will my heart stop bleeding?

1
WHY?

My complaint is still bitter today.
I groan because God's heavy hand is on me.
I wish I knew where to find God
so I could go to where He lives.
I would present my case before Him and fill my mouth
with arguments.
I would learn how He would answer me
And would think about what He would say.

Job 23:1-5, New Century Version

Why God? Why did you let this happen to me? I thought
you were a loving God. Why would you allow this sorrow,
this destruction and this confusion into my life? I feel like I
have been duped, all those years of striving to be a good
woman, praying to you, believing in you, and now this? Who
are you really? Do you in fact exist? Do you actually care
about the broken and lost people of this world? Do you care
about me? I do not know what to believe anymore.

All I know is that the life that I had known for twenty-two years was shattered in a matter of a few seconds as the words of betrayal fell from my husband's confessing lips. How could it be that the man that I had married no longer exists? The memories that I had cherished over those many years were now tainted and stained, no longer fond. My mind convulsed with questions of what had been real in my life and what had been a lie. The excruciating heartache and grief that followed as a result of my husband's choices and the cruel numbness of despair that had taken me hostage would reside with me for months. I wondered whether I would survive this nightmare. The journey through this unknown territory would stretch me beyond what I thought I could bear.

If someone had asked me before what my worst nightmare was, I believe that I would have answered differently. I might have said that the death of my spouse or losing one of my children in a horrific accident or illness would be the worst thing that could happen. Or I might even have said that losing my home to a fire or to a natural disaster would be dreadfully horrible.

After watching the aftermath of hurricane Katrina, the catastrophic desolation to human life and the unbelievable destruction of whole communities, I cannot even imagine a loss of that magnitude. I am thankful that I have not had to experience those tragedies in my life. I pray I never have to be acquainted with the unbearable pain of burying a child.

I did, however, have disturbing nightmarish thoughts that would, on occasion, occupy my mind: *"What if my husband were ever unfaithful to me? How would I respond?"* Those unsettling thoughts would create a sudden panic deep in my heart. I would often become overwhelmed with uncertainty and then quickly force the intruding thought away. I managed to convince myself that my husband loved me, that he was trustworthy and that he would never do that to our family, to us.

I lived my life in what seemed complete normalcy. I tried to be a good wife and mother; I did my best to be a helpmate and encourager to my husband. I failed miserably at times. In the early years we were a normal family—whatever normal means. We went on vacations, we had family dinners, and my husband and I had date nights. Yet as the years progressed, always hidden in the cavernous areas of my restless mind, I had an instinctual awareness that something was not quite right. But I dared not explore what might be causing me to question my husband's fidelity.

For years, I had feared that my husband would be unfaithful to me. Now, I know my intuitions were driving those thoughts. But I chose to ignore the signs. Why would I choose to disregard the red flags? Fear drove my blindness—fear of the truth, fear of what it would mean about me, fear of what the discovery of an affair would do to my future. I feared for my security and my children. Because my husband was a minister, I couldn't face what people in our community would think.

I can now say that living through the devastating aftermath of an unfaithful spouse has been my worst nightmare. The destruction that my betraying husband brought into our home is indescribable. My husband's infidelity destroyed our family's life, as we had known it. Because he was a minister we lost his income, our health insurance, our retirement savings, our home, and many of our friends.

If your spouse has confessed or was caught in an emotional or sexual affair, you know what it is to have to live in the wasteland of rejection and despair. Dread now consumes your life. Or you may be a person who has concerns that infidelity could be in your future. Maybe your intuitions are screaming at you, perhaps you are dismissing the subtle red flags that are flapping you in the face. I understand. I hid behind a veil of fear for years and disregarded the warning signs that frequently waved before me.

I pray that, as you stumble and fall through the debris of your spouse's unfaithfulness, my story can be of some comfort to you. Many people will try to soothe your shattered spirit, but will often fall short. Soon after my husband's confession, I had a caring person try to console me by stating, "At least he did not die like my husband did; you still have him with you. Death is much more difficult to bear than unfaithfulness." I disagreed. The pain of knowing that your spouse has deliberately touched, kissed, or been sexually intimate with another person and shared together a secret life is utterly devastating. The meals, the hotel rendezvous, late night or daytime internet conversations, or hitting pornographic sites to try to satisfy or medicate his emotional needs—I believe those at times can be more than anyone can bear. Then, heap on top of those crimes of the heart, your and your family's many losses because of your spouse's choices. I know it was much more difficult to move forward and to learn how to survive all of that, than if my husband had died. Yes, for me, his death would have been much less cruel. Death is final. You mourn your losses, your dreams, and the fact that you will never feel his heart beat next to yours, or see his beautiful eyes again. But you never have to look into the face of the one who deceived your love and constantly wonder, "*Why, why did you do this to me?*" You never have to lie next to him when the moon casts its eerie glow across his sleeping body and wonder how many nights someone else was in your lover's arms. You never speculate about how often he fantasized about a tryst with the other lover. You never have to wonder about likely images of porn that have been imprinted in his mind.

I do not mean to minimize the death of a loved one. I can only imagine how difficult it would be to recover from that. But having survived his affair, I cannot believe that my pain over his unfaithfulness was easier than if I had lost him to death. I will never suggest death to anyone as a fair comparison.

Now What?

At the time of my emotional and physical collapse on hearing those revolting words, "I have been unfaithful to you," I was desperate for answers to my heart's cry. "*What do I do now? How do I get through this tragedy? Who will walk through this with me?*" I wanted someone with similar experience to tell me what to do, someone who could tell me whether all the emotional craziness I was feeling was normal or not.

My counselor tried to assure me that the wide range of roller coaster emotions that I was experiencing was typical and was a part of the natural process for healing from such a devastating event. But that assurance was not enough, not in the beginning, at least for me. I needed more. Unfortunately I didn't even know what I needed, so for a time I floundered miserably in my confused state of mind.

During the first few weeks after my husband's disclosure I desperately tried to learn how to live this new life. Feelings of emptiness, overwhelming sorrow, and isolation consumed every sleeping and waking moment. A sense of being lost in a dark, terrifying wilderness of despair with no way out became my life now. Confusing emotions continually harassed my mind. I wanted to know whether it was healthy or unhealthy to hate my husband beyond the ends of the earth and to wish that he had died.

Then suddenly, as if someone simply flipped a switch, I would feel intense feelings of love and compassion. I wondered whether the powerful thoughts of wishing that the other person involved would die and be condemned to hell for her part in my husband's betrayal were okay. I wanted her to suffer like I was. Was it odd or just plain crazy to want to have sex so soon after my husband's confession, even though I despised him intensely? What was wrong with me for even having those desires? I felt so unsure of who I was, now that my world had exploded into a thousand fragmented pieces. I wanted to run away from all the responsibilities of motherhood and life. I felt I couldn't handle one more thing, one more task.

Why, why did I think I had to know all the details of their trysts? And how many details would be enough? Repulsive images would literally leave me weak and vulnerable to the constant insecure thoughts of my own unworthiness and shame. I felt I could die of a broken heart.

I became angry with God. I blamed God for my unfortunate life and wondered why God would allow me such pain and misery.

All night long I reach out my hands.
But I cannot be comforted. When I remember God,
I become upset. When I think, I become afraid.
You keep my eyes from closing.
I am too upset to say anything. I keep thinking
about the old days, the years of long ago.
At night I remember my songs.
I think and I ask myself? Will the Lord reject me forever?
Will he be kind to me again? Is His love gone forever?
Has he stopped speaking for all time?
Has God forgotten mercy?
Is he too angry to pity me?

Psalm 77:2-9, New Century Version

Couldn't God have stopped this from happening? Did God not think about the ramifications on my family? If God did not care about me, then fine; but didn't God want what was best for my boys? Their lives were dangling by a very thin thread. How could a good God want that? I felt as if we were all doomed, our lives were forever altered, damaged. My frustration and disappointment in God would go on for a very long time.

Bleeding Heart

Night times would become a haunting dread. If I slept, my dreams would be filled with horrible re-runs of their trysts; and when I could not sleep the constant companion of insecurity and despair would never leave my side. The frequent nag of hunger pains would torment me, but I had no desire for food. I would find it difficult to muster up the energy to fix a meal, so I would rely on a scoop of peanut butter and a glass of milk to sustain me.

I needed help; I needed hope for an uncertain future. This nightmare seemed never ending. I needed guidance.

Perhaps you, too, know something of what I am sharing. You have lost many nights of sleep and you either medicate your pain with food or you have nearly starved yourself because you cannot eat. Your impulsive fear, like that of a frightened cat with its hair standing on ends, keeps you on edge. The range of your emotions can change as quickly as the sun sets into the horizon. One emotion rapidly morphs into another emotion. The swift changes can wreak havoc to your nervous system and your rational functioning.

In her book *After the Affair*, Janis Spring, Ph. D., gives a detailed assessment of the shock to the body during this catastrophic time. She writes:

> As adrenaline and other stress-related hormones pour into your sympathetic nervous system, you experience a heightened state of arousal. You're constantly on the lookout for signs that your partner is straying again. Chronically anxious and agitated, you take longer to fall asleep, awaken frequently during the night, and are more sensitive to noise. You become exhausted from sleeping too little and thinking entirely too much.
>
> Your mind is punctured by vivid and upsetting memories, sensations, and images. When you are asleep, the quality of your dreaming becomes more violent and alarming. When

you are awake you find yourself suddenly lost or disoriented ... Because of alterations to your nervous system, your intense emotions may overwhelm you with a sense of terror and helplessness ...

Another, very different physiological change takes place with the release of endogenous opioids, similar to morphine, into your nervous system. This dulls your perception of pain and shields you from extreme emotional stress. In other words, your body constricts, goes into hibernation, and shuts down. Your range of feelings and sensations narrows, and you lose interest in relationships and activities that only weeks before gave you pleasure and purpose. As you pull yourself together you find yourself barely functioning. Your mind wanders. You have trouble concentrating. Having lost confidence in yourself in your ability to interact with the world, you shrink back into yourself, into isolation. You feel oddly numb and detached ...[1]

When I read Dr. Spring's description of what my husband's affair did to my mind and body I was somewhat relieved. It helped me to know that all of my crazy thoughts, feelings and physical reactions were normal. I felt like I was literally going through what some describe as hell on earth. I often wondered whether the constant affliction of my body and mind would ever go away. I worried about possible future diseases because of the continuous stress from a wound such as this. I wondered if my heart would ever stop feeling like it had been ripped into shreds and trampled on repeatedly. Would the ache always be a part of me? Would my heart ever stop bleeding?

Then without warning, just when I thought that I might be able to pull my life together, cunning mind games would creep in and chaotic madness would invade my emotional well-being. Once again I would question my sanity.

I remember one of those insane episodes a few weeks after my husband confessed. I found myself aimlessly driving down the highway into town, not even sure how I got from point A to point B. The traffic light turned red and I pulled to a gradual stop behind an older white Chevy pick-up truck. With sunglasses concealing my tear-swollen eyes I gazed off into nowhere, which was something I often did as I struggled to survive the constant assault on my mind— my husband's betrayal consuming my every thought. During those moments as I sat and waited for the light to turn green, uncontrollable thoughts erupted. I caught myself secretly looking at the man in front of me through his rear view mirror, my tinted eyewear hiding my stare. I could only see a portion of his face; his dark eyes were staring back at me. I wondered in that moment whether he thought I was attractive. I wondered whether anyone would ever love me or was I destined for this life of despair and sadness forever? I then began fantasizing how I would flirt with the man who stared back at me. Could I let go of all my inhibitions and ride off into the sunset with this stranger in front of me? *"Could I possibly do it? Did I dare?"* I so desperately wanted to feel what it would be like to be touched romantically by another man, to feel the rush that my husband had felt. In that brief moment I tried to imagine what it would be like to have an affair and discard the vows that I had made twenty-two years before. I wondered and even smiled at the thought of how my husband would react to such objectionable behavior. In my mind, I was enjoying the spiteful taunt, *"How does this make you feel now, me in the arms of another man?"*

Just as quickly as that fantasy ignited in my mind, mental aerobics once more began robbing me of my ability to think clearly. I suddenly exploded with anger. My quickened emotional outburst must have caused my face to flush; the redness that surrounded my eyes now joined the heated blush that covered my face and chest. I was livid! I began to think that every man on planet earth was as deceiving and untrustworthy as my husband had been. I furiously glanced around and glared at every driver in every car that was waiting for the signal to change. I began to wonder what his or her secrets were. How many homes were going to be destroyed because of their devious lives? I shook my head as the light turned green, trying to shake the loathsome thoughts away. I continued on my purposeless drive to nowhere, resolving in that moment that I would never again trust my heart to anyone.

2

THE WILDERNESS AHEAD

Get up, God! Are you going to sleep all day?
Wake up!
Don't you care what happens to us?
Why do you bury your face in the pillow?
Why pretend things are just fine with us?
And here we are—flat on our faces in the dirt,
held down with a boot on our necks.
Get up and come to our rescue. If you love us so much,
Help us!

Psalm 44:25-26, The Message

Unfamiliar Terrain

My August 2001 nightmare had become my reality. My heart was sliced wide open by the grotesque claws of betrayal, causing it to bleed for months on end. I felt I was dying a slow agonizing death of abandonment and despair.

After my husband's confession, the regional executive supervisor, where my husband was the senior pastor, personally announced my husband's termination to the congregation, and later in the privacy of our home he stipulated that we were to have no contact with any members or small groups in which we had participated. We were literally severed from our friendships and our support. The friends who did try to be sympathetic had to face their own anger toward my husband and begin their personal journeys toward healing because they had trusted him as their minister.

We were fugitives, sent away emotionally naked. There was no rehabilitation option. We were two wounded people left to survive with no employment, no network of close friends, and no offer of marital therapy or professional restoration. We were excommunicated and wounded. What would happen to our family and our marriage? We left—the two of us with our trust exploded, with three teenage sons who were plagued with their own feelings of confusion and fear of what was to come, and unprocessed anger at their father's behavior.

Because of my shame-filled wounds from my husband's unfaithfulness, I dared not contact anyone in our community. As a result, in the early days I had no one to talk to, to share with or to cry with. My only respite was the once-a-week session with my counselor. When I could not take the raging torment anymore, I would call one of my two dear friends who lived in another state. My journals became a safe refuge for my mind as I expressed my regrets and my sorrows. They were quickly filled with raw and vulnerable emotions as I vented about my anger and my fears.

As I desperately tried to survive the dark, frightening, lonely chaos of my new life, I wished I had been able to read about the journey of someone who had gone before me. I would have been helped to find that their fears were legitimate, that their anger at God was normal, that their feelings of hate were a natural result of a trauma such as ours, and their struggles with understanding forgiveness could take a very long time. I wished that I could have read about a decision that had aided the wounded one. I would have appreciated a confession of a behavior or action that they found themselves regretting as they continued on their pathway to recovery and restoration.

As I documented my thoughts and feelings, I felt a tug on my heart to be willing to publish what I wrote so others could read about my journey on a day-to-day basis. I thought that maybe my passage through this wasteland could be a road map or guide that described the rocky and treacherous terrain of their upcoming journey. I believed that if I shared my story, others could navigate through their own confusing and frightening life and yes, they could survive this tormenting nightmare of betrayal and heartbreak.

As I contemplated writing this survival guide, I often said to myself, "*What can I possibly say to help others in their pain?*" I also had one nagging thought that would hinder me for months and almost quench the desire I had to share my pain with others. I had tremendous fear of sharing the intimate parts of my story. Did I dare share my private journals, my sacred words that flowed from my heart and described my journey? Could I be that vulnerable to readers I had never met—total strangers? What would people think about me? What would they think about my husband?

But courage and I won. So I pressed on, climbing and crawling over and through all hindrances of my mind and the real life circumstances that seemed to try to prevent me from finishing this quest.

I was compelled to share my journey of survival and, if possible, offer a lifeline of hope and comfort. I wanted to be an encourager to the brokenhearted. Maybe I could be a voice of hope during the sleepless nights of those whose dreams have been shattered, who are now on the same path, which I had stumbled alone.

I envisioned that this book would be a conversation. I imagined in my mind that I would meet with the hurting faithful at a local coffee shop sipping hot beverages together. As raw emotions dripped from their injured hearts, these dear wounded would ask with damp eyes and quivering voice, "How did you do it? How did you survive your nightmare?"

I would share, that for me, the second that my husband confessed his unfaithfulness, it was like I had been hurled violently into an unknown wilderness filled with intimidating fear, unfamiliar anger, deplorable shame and isolation. I would share about the terrifying twists and turns that left me exposed and emotionally naked, or the painful mistakes that I made which left me hanging from despairing cliffs of depression and dread. I would describe how I navigated the numerous intimidating pathways along my wilderness journey. I would describe how, out of sheer perseverance and determination, I gained a better understanding of my circumstances and boldly moved forward to the next leg of my journey. I would share the tips that I had learned about the healing processes of recovery that had worked for me, how I chose to learn from my discoveries, and how those difficult decisions would empower me to survive the next minute, hour, or day. I then imagined that, because we shared a common thread of heartache and grief, they would want to know the rest of my story, the whole story. How did it all begin? How did I learn to trust when the voice of doubt screamed louder than the whisper of conviction? How did I survive the unrelenting storms of abandonment and sorrow that seemed to pursue me throughout my whole life? How did I survive my nightmare of an unfaithful spouse?

Believe In Hope

Before any of the "How did I?" questions could be answered, and before I could even think that I could possibly survive my nightmare or consider forgiving the one who had forsaken my love, I had to grasp for hope. Hope gave me the ability to expect a new future. Hope gave me the strength of mind to endure this trauma. These powerful surges of hope were the driving force behind my determination to survive. I became a woman who learned that I had more courage than I thought possible. I faced the dark circumstances that clouded and distorted my reasoning. Hope cleared my head and did this for me. I found and held on tightly to the mighty power of hope, believing that maybe, just maybe, I could have the life that I had always dreamed of. I believe hope can make this possible for anyone.

One of the discoveries that changed my life forever was when I came to the understanding that I was not a victim of my life circumstances. That meant that I had the freedom to choose whether to be another casualty of the betrayed and the wounded, or to move on to the life that was waiting for me. I have to tell you that I actually discovered that I was unconsciously, and at other times very consciously, playing the "victim role." That strategy hindered me from moving forward in my life. When I saw and owned that "victim role" tendency, it became a very important step in my climb toward health. I learned that I could choose to move forward in my pain or not. I could choose to love or not. I could choose to forgive or not. Choosing to trust again would be my greatest challenge.

Have I achieved all of this? Even now, years later, I have more to work on, more discoveries to make. I expect to be on this path toward healing for the rest of my life. I have not arrived, but because of hope I will never give up.

> *Journal Entry, August 20, 2008*
>
> *I am healing; but I believe the trauma of my husband's infidelity will have lasting imprints ... As I have continued to pursue the call on my life to write about my journey I often thought I had to be finished with my healing to be a wounded healer—that I had to know what it looked like at the end of the story—to coach others along their journey. I realize I only need to be one step ahead of the dear people who will be following my footsteps. I must continue to work on my recovery; if I have it all together, (or seem to have it all together) I would lose my authenticity. I feel I must never forget where I came from, or how I arrived at each place of my recovery ...*

I know that you may be in the midst of trying to shake yourself awake from your nightmare. The shock of your spouse's actions and the anguish that it caused consumes your every thought. Before your dreams and life were shattered, my agonizing prayers have already gone out for you as this survival guide took shape. I worked hard to complete this book to help you as you follow in my steps and begin stumbling through the rubble and destruction of an unfaithful partner. You were in my thoughts day and night as I purged my own soul and relived my nightmare over and over to harvest what I had learned and then to get it into print.

Please know that as you read about my journey and how I survived my worst nightmare that I do not pretend to have all of the answers. I struggled and fought to overcome the many obstacles that hindered my journey toward the life I desired. I found that God did not abandon me in spite of venting my anger at His uncertain ways. I learned that, if I let God lead me, God would be my trustworthy Guide.

I am a woman who wants to believe that in sharing my story I might help provide a light of hope through your dark night as you are traumatized and your life's dreams crash. Just maybe my story can bring a glimmer of hope to you in your shattered and broken world.

I believe that is why any of us must survive our nightmares. We need to be quiet voices who weep with other broken hearts, helping the hopeless to believe again, to believe in themselves, maybe even for the first time. Through this story of my survival I set out to come alongside the lost one who is stumbling along the same dark and blinding path of betrayal. I want to be a voice of hope and encouragement. Survivors can call back and encourage the faithful to be willing to trust again, to trust in the one, who is guiding them, to believe that there is a life waiting for them. That is why we must survive!

If you have gone a little way ahead of me, call back—
it will cheer my heart and help my feet along the stony track;
and if, perhaps, faith's light is dim, because the oil is low,
your call will guide my lagging course as wearily I go.

Call back, and tell me that *God* went with you
into the storm; call back, and say He kept you when the
forest's roots were torn; that when the heavens thunder
and the earthquake shook the hill He born you up and
held you where the lofty air was still.

Oh friend, call back, and tell me for I cannot see your face;
they say it glows with triumph, and your feet sprint
in the race ...

But if you'll say *God* heard you when your prayer was but
a cry, and if you'll say He saw you through the night's
sin-darkened sky, if you have gone a little way ahead,
O friend, call back—it will cheer my heart and help
my feet along the stony track.

Author Unknown (*Italics Mine*)

❤ HEART WORK

From day one I had intense feelings and yet, at times I had difficulty giving names to them. I was angry, sad, or depressed. Beyond those few "feeling" words, I didn't think I could express and document my emotions. To help with my frozen state of mind, my counselor gave me a list of feeling words. I would look over the list and choose the word or words that best described my state of mind in that moment. If you too find that you struggle with locating and naming your feelings, in the Appendix there is a list of feeling words to help you.

What you think and how you feel will be in conflict for a while; don't try to make sense of all the confusion right now. Truth will come; but today, you NEED to FEEL. Begin to write your feelings down as if no one will ever read them. You can start by writing, "What do I feel today? I feel_____." Then just let your feelings flow; try your best to identify at least three emotions. Getting your feelings onto paper where they can be seen and validated is an important first step in preparing your heart for healing.

It is important to understand that you did not choose these feelings and feelings are not to be labeled or judged. Feelings left buried are a breeding ground for more pain and unresolved issues.

3
How Did I Get Here?

I believe we have two lives,
the life we learn with, and the life we live after that.

Quote from the movie, *The Natural*

Sometimes a person has to go back, really back—to have
a sense, an understanding of all that's gone to make
them—before they can go forward.

Paule Marshall

November 2002: One year and three months after my August nightmare terrorized my sleep.

How did I get here? I gaze at the blue, green, and grey patterned walls; the carpet is Mediterranean Sea blue, a beautiful blue, but not my taste in floor coverings. The kitchen is rather large but there is not enough cupboard space to store my plates, pots and pans, or food. I have

23

put many items in a storage unit and the local second-hand store received boxes and bags of my life collections and memories. Not just kitchen items, but half of my previous life is now gone to some other home; a stranger now sleeps in my sheets, wears my clothes and so proudly says, "I only paid $3.00 for it, what a bargain!" It is a sad, sad thought of how many untold stories are on display at the many thrift shops around the world. Someone's life has changed, either by his or her own choice or by the choices of others.

It is late fall, almost Thanksgiving. I don't feel thankful at all. Yes, I am glad I have a place to lay my head at night, but I do not sleep much. I have food on my shelves and I have a car to drive. I have all of my basic needs taken care of, yet I stare at these permanently wallpapered mobile home walls and again ask the question: "How did I get here?"

It wasn't long ago, six weeks exactly, that I was floating on a florescent pink blow-up raft, sipping a homemade iced vanilla latté in my beautiful swimming pool, enjoying a quiet, peaceful Saturday afternoon.

I loved my former home. We had purchased it two years prior when my husband accepted the position of senior pastor in the college town where we had first met. We were so excited to be moving back to our old stomping grounds.

The moment I stepped through the front door I knew, *"This is it, this is our new home!"* It was my dream house, with generously appointed dark cherry wood floors and cabinets and custom trim work throughout. It had a large master suite with a garden tub and French doors that opened out to a patio that surrounded the in-ground swimming pool. The yard was beautifully landscaped with decorative rocks, mature trees and shrubs, and the water feature next to the pool created a calm and relaxing atmosphere. A gorgeous view of the mountains and a lake was just beyond the borders of our property.

But now, in a matter of days, my life as I knew it had been brutally displaced. We had to give up our beautiful home because we no longer had an income to sustain the monthly payments. We moved into a tiny borrowed manufactured home out in the middle of nowhere to try to recover from my husband's devastating choices. No grass, no trees, no life. Only dirt, weeds and rocks scattered the landscape. The barrenness and bleakness of my new living arrangement only intensified the feeling of emptiness and sadness that now consumed my whole being.

I had had great dreams. Dreams of a healthy, fulfilling marriage and of a contented family, but many detours and obstacles altered those aspirations. And now, here I sit in depressing isolation, in what seems to be a hopeless situation.

From early on my life had always had its challenges. I believe a strong and determined will slithered out with me as the doctor guided my tiny frame from my mother's womb. Somewhere along my journey I learned that, in order for me to survive the assaults on my life, I had to begin to dig deeply into the dark caverns of my mind and unearth the fragmented pieces of my past. In doing so I would begin to mourn for the first time the many losses of my childhood and adult life. I believe it was only through my willingness to push and at times crawl through the challenging issues that for so long had held my mind captive that I would gain enough confidence to navigate bravely into my present and learn how to survive my current nightmare—my husband's infidelity.

So, once again I wonder, how is it that I could not seem to outrun the terrorizing beasts of my dreams? How did I get so lost, so confused? Why did my husband have to hurt me so brutally, so deeply?

How did I get here?

———

My Story

My story begins at birth on a frigid winter day that seems not long ago. I imagine that my father paced back and forth on a spotlessly clean linoleum floor that covered an entire floor of a hospital wing, the smell of ammonia wafting throughout the room. As I visualize my birth day, I see a strapping young man in his mid-twenties continuing to march from one end of the room to the other. He probably glanced often towards the heavy steel swinging doors that led to the forbidden zone, the place where only expectant mothers, the doctors and the trained nurses belonged.

In my mind's eye I see my father waiting and pacing for what seemed to be an eternity. I am sure he was concerned that the delivery was taking too long, but submitting to the fact that he had no control over the situation, he would relieve his mind by perusing the collection of magazines that were neatly arranged on a small end table in the waiting room. My Dad would probably have picked up the latest issue of the National Geographic—one of his favorite periodicals, I would learn as I grew up. I then envision him sitting down on one of the firm vinyl sofas that were scattered around the room and flipping each page in an involuntary manner. His mind, I am sure, was occupied with thoughts of my mother and me. *"Will I have another son or will I be blessed with a daughter?"*

As I conjure up this day in my mind, I picture Dad just beginning to rest his weary legs when a nurse dressed in a finely pressed white uniform came rushing through the double doors to give him the news, "Congratulations, you are a proud father of a beautiful, healthy, baby girl!" Then she dashed back behind the steel barrier and down the long corridor to attend to my mother and her new arrival.

This is how I imagine my birth, the day I took my first breath, suckled my mother's breast, and felt my father's gentle arms as he cuddled me close to his warm, strong body. All this took place in an old brick and mortar building on a cold winter day.

I had started life just like everyone else: Mom's labor pains, the pushing, the spanking, and the first cry. I am sure my parents were thrilled to finally hold their new, sweet bundle of joy. In that moment life seemed so perfect, so right, for a time.

My Earilest Memories

I might have been a year and a half old, maybe two; I am not sure. All I remember is that I was wearing a pretty pink dress, and I had a very special job to do. I was to walk in front of this beautiful woman in a long, white gown. After standing beside her I remember walking outside the building and falling down on something very slippery—small white pebbles or something. As I grew older I realized that I had slipped and fallen on the rice that had been thrown on the steps of the church to celebrate the departure of the new husband and wife.

I can vividly see in my memory the brown pews, the bland white walls and the rough wooden beams that ran across the ceiling. I can recall the scrape on my knee and my mother tenderly comforting me and wiping the tears from my cheek.

My next earliest memory was when a family from our church invited our family over for dinner. I remember sitting at a round dining room table and being so small that I could barely reach my plate, my feet sticking straight out. I can recall not feeling very comfortable with my seating arrangement and I remember the adults talking for what seemed like hours and hours. I remember that I had to go potty, so I asked for permission to leave the table. I followed the host's instructions and got myself to the bathroom. As I finished my business, I reached up to flush and noticed a piece of gum that had been torn in half on the toilet tank lid. I was maybe four years old at the time. I knew that taking that stick of gum was wrong, but I wanted it. Why I didn't just put that gum in my mouth right then and there I will never know. Maybe I knew that my parents would see me chomping on it and would have scolded me in front of everyone. So, I had to come up with an alternative plan. My little dress had a belt that was sown on. It conveniently had an opening in the top of the belt that was a perfect place to hide something, like a piece of gum. So I safely tucked it away, to chew at a later time. I never got the opportunity to taste the sweet juicy treat.

Just like all children seem to do, I had forgotten about my earlier heist and later that evening, as my mother was helping me take off my dress, my tasty treat fell to the floor. My mother looked at me with such shock, and in a condemning tone asked, "Where did you get this?" I was filled with so much guilt. I explained where I found the gum and tried to justify to my parents why I would steal from church people. I remember feeling so small, and my parents were these intimidating giants, critical and harsh. I was spanked and put to bed.

The next day was Sunday and I had been instructed that I would return the stolen gum to the church people and tell them that I was sorry for stealing. Even as I write that memory down, I am torn. Did my parents respond correctly in that situation? Was it necessary for me to feel such guilt and shame over a half stick of gum? Maybe so. I never again had the thought to steal another thing.

It is amazing what kids remember, what stays lodged in our memory banks forever.

Childhood Messages

There are a few memories of my childhood that I desperately wish I could forget. One of those painful memories will be embedded in my mind for the rest of my life. The ramifications of this event have altered my life forever and even as an adult I have struggled with the messages that were so blatantly taught on that early spring day.

I was in the first grade. This particular day was bright and sunny. My class had just come in from noon recess and it was almost time for Show and Tell. I was very excited because it was my day to share and I had brought my favorite dolly. I couldn't wait to pull her out of the paper sack in which I had so carefully placed her. I was anticipating my classmates' expressions of envy as they oohed and aahed over my most prized possession.

Shortly after we came in from playing outside and just before my teacher called her class to the large, multi-colored rug for Show and Tell, my mother peeked in the door of my classroom. In retrospect she looked a bit anxious, but as a little girl I was not capable of truly sensing those kinds of emotions. I was just excited to see her and I ran to give her a hug. I overheard her tell my teacher that I would be leaving for a few days and asking her for some homework assignments so that I would not get behind in class. I quickly grabbed my jacket and papers and left with my mother.

Elated by my early release, I hurriedly jogged alongside my mother, trying to keep up with her large quick strides as we exited the school and headed toward the parking lot. I asked her with great anticipation where we were going and she said harshly, "On vacation."

She did not offer any more explanation. I asked excitedly, "Where?"

Mother hurriedly sat me next to my waiting brother in the backseat of our four-door, light green sedan, and again she responded with a short answer, "Oregon."

As Mother climbed in behind the steering wheel, I continued to bombard her with inquiries. "Where is Daddy? Isn't he coming on vacation, too?"

Her response, in a more irritated tone, "He is at work" and "No, Daddy is not coming with us."

Confused, but delighted all at the same time, I continued to probe her with never ending questions.

Mother drove away from the school parking lot. Soon we were on the highway heading somewhere without my Daddy. As I sat low in the back seat and stretched my neck to peer out the window, a sudden shock of horror raced through my little body. I realized that I had left my dolly at school and cried out to my mother, "My dolly, my dolly, we have to go back and get my dolly!"

It seemed that Mother was at the point of exasperation by my constant chatter and now with my continuous cries for my doll, she could take it no more and shouted at me, "No! We are not going back to get your doll, now do not say another word until I tell you that you can!"

Mother's choice of words stung my heart as much as if she had slapped my fragile face. Crushed, heartbroken and confused, I did as she said. Crying softly, I leaned my head against the thin, green padding of the car door and allowed the low hum and vibration of the engine to lull me into an unwanted slumber.

Mother drove for hours, the final destination still unclear. As the sun began to set, my mother pulled into a motel parking lot and rented a room for the night. Still sulking from the events of the day, I quietly ate my dinner, crawled into my rented bed, alone, without my favorite dolly to comfort me as I tried to fall asleep in a strange and lonely place.

I am not sure how much time had elapsed, but something aroused me from my slumber. The motel room was dark except for the glow of the light through the bathroom door that had been left ajar. I was scared. I needed my mother, so I groped my way across the room to my mother's connecting door.

I quietly open her door and, as the brightness from the bathroom cast a shaft of light across my mother's bed, I found her not alone, but with a naked man. The man was not Daddy.

As my eyes adjusted to the appalling sight that was before me and as the nude man jumped out of the motel bed and ran for cover in the shadows, my unclothed mother, now standing right in front of me, screamed, "You are a bad, bad girl!"

Six-year-old children are not supposed to know how to deal with the shock of seeing their mother in bed, naked, with a family friend. I am not sure whether what happened next was because of what I had just witnessed or if it was the reason for my getting up in the middle of the night and opening the adjoining room door. But as my mother's screams echoed in my head I quickly turned and desperately tried to make it to the toilet. I missed and ended up vomiting on the yellowish, stained bathroom floor.

I should have been at home sound asleep in my own bed, with my favorite dolly, safe and secure. But instead, that event (and how I, the little girl, perceived the experience of that night) would be a trauma that would scar and inform the rest of my life.

For the next two weeks my mother continued her trek of running from her previous life and trying to start a new life with her lover. I really don't know all of the details that surrounded those events. But I do know that it took my father those two weeks to find us and convince my mother that her life would be better with him. We were back home once again and all I wanted was for us to be a happy family. Life would never be the same for a little girl who now knew too much and had no tools for understanding the episode at all.

Don't Open That Door

Silly as it may seem, the message that was embedded in my young memory, "*You are a bad girl if you open doors!*" would have a horrific grip on me for years. I had consciously learned from that childhood incident in that dingy motel room that, if I opened doors—not physical doors, but emotional doors—I would be making a huge mistake. If I opened doors, bad things would happen, which would reinforce the deep-rooted message that "I am bad."

How does a grown woman go about her life not opening doors? I would isolate myself from any close relationships for fear that they might betray me. I would refuse to confront issues. Instead, I would hide behind them. I didn't dare ask questions. I would pretend not to notice.

I became a well-worn rug that everyone could walk on and, as a result of being a fine piece of floor covering—I looked pretty "together" on the outside; oh, the masks that I wore—I learned to stuff and hide my feelings. I was very careful not to shake out any of the accumulated emotional dirt and grime for fear of what might be exposed about me. Eventually these practices would numb my ability even to give names to my feelings. Through the years the numbing effects of my emotional brokenness began to take its toll on me. I would often buckle under the weight of personal and relational insecurities. Low self-worth was my constant companion. As a result, those closest to me had little or no respect for me as well. My husband and my children would be first on the list to treat me badly.

I was held captive, and fear was my abductor. Opening any emotional doors would make me too vulnerable. I had to protect myself from any more heartache and pain.

All of these behaviors would prevent me from facing reality and keep the emotional doors closed, which then allowed me to choose to be alone. Being alone and isolated felt like the safest and most protected way to live. Self-protection became my method of choice for survival.

As a child, I learned how to live that self-protected life. I never told anyone what I saw that night in that dark, grimy motel room. Nor did I tell anyone about the many other rendezvous meetings I had witnessed over the next six years between my mother and that man who was not her husband.

Years of stormy days and nights would follow that dark and confusing event. During the chaos of those years two more siblings were born into my family. My father had to travel some for his job and as a result there would be many nights that my mother would leave me home alone to care for my little brothers while she went out to meet her friend. I clearly remember those nights when she was away. I felt I had to be responsible, and yet I had so much fear. How could a mother leave a child with such little boys? I had to persevere. I had no choice in the matter. I worked hard at being the best big sister that I could be.

It is amazing how one night in a motel room many years before could produce so many wrong messages and cause me to develop a strategy to live out my life in such isolation, such confusion. I lived with these mistaken thoughts until just a few years ago when I realized how those false beliefs had wounded my life and had been the driving force behind my poor choices.

Seasons Without Storms

There would be seasons when the clouds of despair and confusion would break apart for a time and the storms of life seemed to cease. During those welcomed periods of respite, I have some wonderful mental snapshots of childhood joys that are comforting as I think back on them.

Among the best times were those when I went hunting and fishing with Dad. I loved spending one-on-one time with him. I remember one day in particular. We got up way before daylight and drove forever to get to that perfect spot. Dad then cleared an area under the aspen groves, and as he organized his hunting equipment I would watch the round leaves dance and flutter. The gentle morning breezes would race through our own little mountain sanctuary. I remember standing under the tree canopy marveling in respectful awe as I witnessed the first morning sun burst through to the forest floor and send a heavenly glow all around me. I felt as if I had just entered into God's garden as the warmth of the sun cast a halo above my head. I felt that I could reach out and touch the angels that hovered above. The smell of the woods waking up from its night slumber was invigorating and refreshing. Even though I was just a little girl I loved the feeling of being in the wild wilderness with my father. It was a magical experience for me.

The night before our excursion I would gather up my collection of dolls and toys to take with me into the woods. I would use the forest foliage for my props and live in this fantasy world of joy and wonder. While I played in my make-believe land, I would talk and talk and talk. My poor Dad would be so patient with me. He wanted to hunt and bring home a deer and make his delicious jerky, but with all my visiting with him and with my dolls there would be no deer, let alone any woodland creature getting within a half a mile of us.

I am not really sure how many times I went hunting, or if I was ever invited again after this one crisp, early fall outing. But having this one wonderful memory of being in the woods with Dad is a treasure that I hold warmly in my heart.

Another early memory that evokes wonderful feelings is the family camping trips to the great Rocky Mountains. We would pack the midnight blue Chrysler station wagon to the brim with all of our camping paraphernalia, and drive for what seemed like hours and hours. Upon arrival at the campground, we would drive around the winding one-way lanes again and again until my mother found the perfect site. My parents would begin to unpack the large collection of camping equipment that had been compressed into our car and recreate a home away from home. They would work skillfully together, like finely tuned machines as they cleared the ground of any rocks and debris. Pitching the smelly, green army tent was always first on the to-do list. Next, they filled the cooler with fresh mountain spring water at one of the many hand water pumps located throughout the camp. They set up the propane cooking stove on one end of the picnic table. Then they spread a checkered tablecloth and tacked it down. They hung the clothes line and set up the folding lawn chairs in a circle around the fire pit.

We were set. I could always boast that our campsite was the best in the whole camp. I knew it because my brother and I would ride our bikes or walk around the campsites, trying not to gawk too much as we sauntered by each of the campers and observed their set-ups.

I am not sure how it happens, but every camping parent knows when it does—a child will reach the age of being mature enough to dip a poker stick into the flames and twirl and dance in the darkness of the night. I remember arriving at that place of maturity and with childlike wonder I would create glowing, swirling displays of fiery red trails that spun and danced magically in the air. This was accompanied, of course, by frequent parental warnings, "Be careful with that hot stick before you burn somebody with it!"

I am enamored even today by the pleasing woodsy aroma of forest logs burning in fire pits, accompanied by the mesmerizing weaving of smoke and sparks that kiss the canopy of trees above. The nightly rituals of roasting hotdogs on chiseled sticks or eating sticky, gooey, marshmallow s'mores brings to my mind heartwarming childhood memories.

Another memory in particular that I love to reflect on is the annual summer vacations to the Oregon coast to visit Uncle Jack and Aunt Nora's dairy farm. Each summer upon my arrival, my uncle would tell me that he had something to show me and, because I knew exactly what it was, I would be ecstatic. I would follow my uncle into the barn to the area where the paddocks held the mother cows just before giving birth to their calves. I just loved dancing anxiously on the wooden railing next to the pen of the laboring cow as I watched my uncle help deliver a baby calf. I remember how the mother cow would relax as my uncle entered the stall; it was clear that she knew it as her signal that it was time to give up the gangly baby that was inside of her. My mind would marvel at how all of those long legs and sharp hooves could be inside of the mother's belly and not hurt her as they thrashed and kicked. As I stood on the railing to get a good view, I would watch in anticipated awe as the cow's bulging belly slowly moved like waves lapping on a shore. I would hold my breath and wrinkle my face in disgust as my uncle inserted his hand inside of the cow to grab the front hooves to help deliver the newborn. What a remarkable moment it was for me to witness this miracle of life.

Every summer on the farm my cousins and I would play hide and seek in the oversized haystack just outside my uncle's barn, ignoring the itchy reaction that our skin would get from the straw. Often times we would take daytrips to the nearby ocean. We would walk for miles, it seemed, looking for perfect seashells and agate rocks. We would build sandcastles on the beach and with childlike faith we thought we could dig to China, only to have our aspirations dashed when the deep cavity quickly filled again with the ocean tide. We would play for hours and hours in our wet and sandy playground until our chilled bodies would beg to be warmed. The day would end with hot soapy baths in my Aunt Nora's funny tub that had strange claw-shaped feet. Our weary little bodies would fall asleep each night listening to the muffled conversations of the adults while old recordings of Johnny Cash played in the background.

Those were magnificent days to be a child. No fears, or worries, no concerns. Oh, if only life could be that simple once again. If I could go back in time, I would cuddle longer with the barnyard kittens. I would muster more courage and jump off the highest rung of the barn ladder onto the waiting hay below. And I would take the wheel of the large and scary tractor when my Uncle offered, overcoming my fear of intimidating farm machinery. If I had known in advance that these precious memories were all I would have, I would have tried to capture more of them.

Most of my childhood and young adult life is like peering into a deep dark cavern. Something is in there, you can feel it, even sense it, but you can't see it. I have very vague recollections of my youthful past. I believe because of the tragic and painful events of my childhood and because of the magnitude of those events, my traumatized memory, to preserve my sanity, has blocked the memories.

I am thankful that I do have a few good memories that I can reminisce over, but many of my years are wiped clean from my memory bank, lost forever. I have often wondered if I will ever remember more details of my past or if I am destined to be captive to my early childhood survival blackout.

❤ Heart Work

Much of what we experience before age twelve seems normal, or not that big of a deal, but much of our belief system comes from what we experienced during those critical years. As you read the pieces of my story, keep your journal close by. Turn to the last five empty pages in your journal and write a heading that reads, "What I Remember." DON'T try to make sense of the memories that may surface as you begin to write in this section. As memories come to you in the next weeks and months, flip to this part of your journal and write them down, as they will prove valuable later.

4
MY REALITY

*Dreams are illustrations ... from the book
your soul is writing about you.*

Marsha Norman

Dreams vs. Reality

As a young girl I had a reoccurring dream. I had a vivid dream a dozen or so times during my elementary school years. I dreamed that I was outside in my front yard standing by a small tree that Dad had just planted. The wind was blowing violently. A massive storm was on its way; you could sense its fierceness. The sky was an eerie swirling orange and grey color, dark and bright at the same time. Not a sound could be heard—no birds chirping, no dogs barking, not even the roar of the highway that was nearby. There was complete silence. I remember looking around. Feeling very anxious, I couldn't see a single person. Mom, Dad and my brother were nowhere to be found. I was all alone and very frightened. The wind began blowing even more intensely and I could see in the distance a strange cloud coming towards me. The sky was so dark; it felt as if this cruel storm was coming to consume me. The force of the wind was so strong that I was beginning to lose my balance. The only thing I could find to hold onto was that little tree that Dad had planted. The sapling was only as tall as I was and about a half an inch in diameter. I grabbed hold of the tiny tree and hung on. The wind was now bearing down on me and I was being tossed around like a flag on a flagpole, holding tightly so as not to be lifted up and hurled across the landscape into the vicious belly of the raging tempest. The storm passed, and as I turned to walk back to my house, I was in shock at what I saw. The roof of my house had been completely blown off. There was no siding or interior walls. The frame of the house was the only part that was left standing. I walked up to the front porch and peered into what just a few minutes before had been the main level. There was no floor left of the house. I could hear someone whimpering and I wiggled my small, limp body through the debris to see who was crying. As I peered down through the broken and mangled lumber that once had been my house, I saw my older brother sitting on the basement floor. He was cut and bleeding from his wounds.

I would always wake up at this time. As a little girl, I had no idea what this all meant. I was even too frightened to tell my parents that I would have this dream over and over. I often thought that I must have been a bad girl to have such terrible dreams, or that something was wrong with me. Little girls should not be so afraid, so alone with their thoughts and their dreams.

42

Could I Survive This Vicious Storm?

I remember that fateful Saturday morning in the fall of 1971. It would be the first day of many to come that the Mother I had known for eleven years would no longer reside in our home.

I walked into the living room to turn on the television to watch my favorite Saturday morning cartoons. As I entered the room I found Mother lying in a fetal position, holding her knees, rocking, crying softly and saying, "Take me to the police! Take me to the police!" I ran down the hallway to their bedroom to get Dad. Within a few minutes my whole family was in our midnight blue Chrysler station wagon driving to the local police station. My three brothers and I were sitting in our nightclothes on a long, well-worn wooden bench looking through a large glass window at Dad having a heated discussion with the police. We had been in such a hurry that the only one who was dressed was Dad. I was wearing a light pink flannel gown and my brothers had on their two-piece hero pajamas. There were several police officers busy at their desks, typing on their typewriters and sipping their coffee.

As I stared through the thick pane of glass, not hearing anything but the sound of footsteps down a distant corridor and a female voice laughing at someone's joke from around the corner, I thought to myself, *"Doesn't anybody care? Something is wrong with my mom. Why does everyone look as if there is nothing wrong here?"* Through the dense glass I could see some of the officers were listening to my frantic father's story and would occasionally look over at us. I can't even imagine how pathetic we must have looked. I am not sure how long we sat in the police station. I can vividly picture Mother on that dreary Saturday morning as she sat slumped in a grey office chair, wearing her robe and slippers, looking very frightened, fragile and all alone, like a lost little girl. That memory will be imprinted in my mind forever.

With dread, we climbed back into the car and headed home, not understanding the events that had just happened and apprehensive about what was to come. The minute we drove into the driveway, Mom started to get hysterical!

She kept saying over and over in a panicked, fretful voice, "Get the bugs out!! Get the bugs out!" She would not allow anyone in the house until Dad made a complete search for any "listening devices." She believed that our home had been literally "bugged." She thought someone was spying on our family, and we were not safe to enter the house.

Within a few hours Dad took Mom to the nearest hospital's psychiatric ward and had her admitted. Many tests were done and within a couple of days the results came back. My mom was diagnosed with multiple personality disorder and paranoid schizophrenia. Within just a few hours, the Mother I once knew no longer existed. The medications she took turned her into a completely different person. There was no longer any life in her beautiful green eyes. She never laughed again, and I don't remember her ever crying again. She would wander the house in her bathrobe and baby blue slippers, hardly speaking a word to anyone. The only person she seemed to recognize was my youngest brother, who was three years old at the time.

During those days we lived a very secluded life. This kind of illness was not talked about much in small towns. We were private people before this tragic event, but now it seemed we were forced into a dark world of isolation and uncertainty. Dad did the best he could to take care of four young children and a wife who was mentally ill, while working a full time job. I cannot even imagine the turmoil he must have had to deal with in his mind, and the daily stress of how he was going to survive this unexpected nightmare.

Winter passed, spring came, and as the crocus and tulips began to emerge, so did my mother. At times it seemed she was getting better. She appeared to be happier and would smile and go about her normal household duties.

However, there was one thing that she did that seemed so strange to me. Mother never slept in her bed anymore. I would wake up in the morning and she was always asleep in my bed. Some things in a child's life do not make any sense at all. I am not sure why, but I never questioned her changed sleeping arrangement.

One morning in late spring Dad came in, kissed her good-bye and left for work. Within a couple of minutes the doorbell rang and she went to answer. Mother did not know, but I followed her. When she opened the door I watched her kiss the man that she had been seeing secretly for more than six years. This was the first time since the night in the motel that I had actually seen them together. I had heard them through the floor register vents on nights that Dad was away and had heard some of her phone conversations, but here, again, I am seeing the betrayal. As a twelve year old, I knew this was not appropriate behavior. I didn't want to be scolded again, so I quickly ran through the kitchen, went downstairs to the laundry room and pretended to be looking for something to wear to school that day. I heard the footsteps coming down the stairs and I held my breath.

Had she seen me? What if she did? What will I do if she starts yelling at me like she did in the motel room six years ago? She came up behind me. I stood frozen, waiting.

There was more life in her eyes than I had seen in a long time. Something was different. This was not the same woman that had been living in our home for months. She had this energy about her and I was frightened. She asked me with an inquisitive voice, "Who was at the door?" I thought it was a strange question. She knew who was at the door; she had just kissed him!

I am not sure, but it was as if I knew that I was not conversing with my mother, but one of her "other personalities." I had never seen the transformation before, nor did I at such a young age really understand her illness, but I believe it was a piece of wisdom that I was to have for the moment. So I lied. I told her that I thought it was the mailman, she said, "Yes, yes, that's who it was," in a rather strange, immature tone and she then quickly turned and went back up the stairs.

I really cannot be sure how much time elapsed between that early morning doorbell encounter and the final ill-fated day my mother was in our home.

It started like most mornings. Father came in my room as usual, kissed my mother good-bye and left for work. As soon as he walked out the door, my mother jumped out of bed and quickly ran through the house gathering suitcases and clothes. I knew immediately what she was doing. She was leaving Dad again. She packed up boxes of clothes for my two little brothers and several times came into my room and stood over my bed to tell me to start packing. Because I remembered what it had been like the first time she left—the confusion, the chaos, the fighting that followed—I wanted nothing to do with it this time. I knew my mom was sick and I was not going to leave Dad again. My Dad represented safety and stability, and I wasn't going to leave home and Dad.

Then the begging began, followed with pleading. When that didn't work, my mother tried to bribe me into leaving. She told me that if I would leave with her, she would buy me all the clothes I've ever dreamed of, if only I would leave with her lover Ken and her. I told Mother I was not leaving my Dad again. She then went on to try to explain why she was leaving Dad, why she loved Ken, that she always loved Ken. I must have questioned her behavior, her affair, because she tried to justify it by telling me, "This is what friends do."

This is not a conversation that a twelve year old should have with her Mother. I heard things and saw things that no young child should ever have to see and hear. It would be many years later before I began to realize the damage of the messages about me that were vividly stamped in my mind.

I got myself ready for school. I could hear her rushing around the house gathering up her belongings. My poor brothers had no idea what was about to happen to them. I did. I had been in their shoes just a few years before. My heart was torn; what was I supposed to do?

I walked to school very slowly, stopping and turning, looking back at my house, hoping that when I got home that afternoon I would find that I had only imagined what had just transpired.

I don't remember the day at school at all; my thoughts were always wandering to the events of the morning. The day seemed never to end.

I rushed home after school as fast as I could, ran into the house looking for signs of my mother and brothers. Nothing. The house was empty, empty of the sounds of little boys playing, or of my mother in the kitchen preparing dinner. It felt cold, abandoned. I walked around that barren home, feeling dizzy and weak from the sudden loss that I felt. I walked outside and sat on the lawn next to the driveway, waiting. I was waiting for Dad, waiting for someone to make sense of this tragic moment. I sat there on the dry lawn, picking blades of grass, running them between my fingers, wondering where she was going this time. How far had they driven in those hours while I was at school? I wondered whether my little brothers could even comprehend the mayhem that was now about to be a part of their young lives forever. Of course not, they were too young for that understanding. But I knew, and I cried for them. I mourned for their inability to stand up and refuse Mother's mentally ill attempt to run away from her sickness.

As cars passed by, I wondered if somebody would notice the forlorn girl sitting all alone. Did they see the tears that ran down my cheeks?

I felt so alone and abandoned—abandoned by a mother and by a world too busy to notice or care.

As I watched Dad's car turn the corner, it was 3:45 P.M. (always the same time every day). My heart was racing. *How do I tell him, what do I say? Do I let him walk into the house and find out for himself?* My mind was so confused; my heart was broken. The pressure was too heavy for a young girl to manage all alone.

As Dad pulled the car into the driveway, he didn't even get a chance to get completely out of his car before I bolted to him. "She's gone!" I screamed, "Mom's gone!"

Dad ran up the porch, into the house and went straight to his bedroom. I followed. It was as if he knew what to look for, as if he'd been in this exact set of circumstances before. As I silently followed him into his room, he took large quick steps to get to Mother's side of the bed. There on her pillow was a letter, folded neatly inside of an envelope.

Reluctantly he removed the pages and began reading the words that had been carefully written in Mother's perfect penmanship. He lowered the pages down to his side and then brought them back up to read again, as if he hadn't read it right the first time.

Dad wailed; the pain and agony in his weeping tore through my soul. He looked at me with tears streaming down his checks, and cried, "You are my daughter, your brothers are my sons, you are my children, I know the day that you all were conceived, you are all mine."

I stood there in that emotionally-dark bedroom, speechless. Blinking back the tears, I looked down and saw Mother's wedding ring lying on the neatly-made bed. She was gone. *My mother was gone and this time I knew it was forever.*

As Dad somberly walked out of the bedroom, I saw the letter lying on the bed next to the ring. I probably shouldn't have, it really wasn't my business, but I picked up the pages of my mother's last words to my father and began reading. She told Dad she never loved him. She said the children were not his, that she was gone and would not be coming back, and not to come after her. There was more, but I think my brain had been so traumatized that the rest of her letter is just a blank page in my memory.

On that emotional dismal and gloomy spring day, not only did I lose Mother, but Dad disappeared as well. His body was present. He went to work, came home, tried to plan and prepare dinners, went grocery shopping, did laundry—but the Dad that I had known, the Father who had been my stability, my safe place, was now a prisoner in a dark world of depression. For years, every night, he would sit in the dark and gaze blankly out of the kitchen window; staring at the pine tree that Mother asked him to plant years before. Mother loved trees. Tears would quietly flow down his face.

I was now totally alone. No Mother, no Father, just an older brother who in his early teen years would escape to his own private world in his bedroom, only coming out to use the bathroom, eat, and go to school. I've often wondered what was going through his mind during those days. He would never talk about it then, and even to this day, he does not want to speak much about that time in our lives.

A little girl's recurring nightmare did come true. My home had been blown to splinters.

She Loves Me, She Loves Me Not

I am not certain how much time elapsed. It felt like an eternity. One morning I was entering my 6th grade classroom. I had just taken off my jacket and hung it on the coat hooks outside of the room and was walking through the doorway, when my friend Kim, who lived across the street from my house, came running down the hall. "Patti, Patti, your Mom's home, your Mom's home!" I didn't even stop to ask questions. I ran as fast as I could to the school office and asked if I could use the phone. The school secretary must have known about the hardships that had fallen on my family; she didn't even ask me why.

I had by now memorized Dad's work phone number and dialed it quickly. When he answered the phone I exclaimed with much excitement and anticipation, "Dad, Mom's home! Kim told me. She saw her drive up in our station wagon and park in the driveway. Mom's home!"

As I hung up the phone I hurriedly ran to the end of the school sidewalk so I could look down the street at my house. My home was only a block away from the school, so I could clearly see it, and yes, Mother's car was in the driveway. Parked behind her was her Ken's ugly brown El Camino. I couldn't believe it! I stood there, waiting. I don't know what I was waiting for, why I didn't run home. Maybe the secretary told me not to leave the school grounds. I am not sure, but I just stood there watching and waiting for something to happen. Within just a few minutes, Dad's white jeep screeched around the corner and before his car came to a complete stop, he jumped out. I watched as he reached into Ken's car and pulled my youngest brother out through the passenger side window. Then I watched him run into the house holding a confused little boy tightly in his arms. I wanted to run home, but as I said, I must have been told to stay on the school property. I stood there for what seemed like a lifetime. Then the bell rang and I reluctantly turned towards the front doors of the school and went to class.

The day dragged. What was happening in my home? Did Mom come back? It was torture sitting in my desk trying to focus on school work when there was something more important going on. Mom was home! Fidgeting with my pencil, I tried to listen to Mr. Scott, my sixth grade teacher, give instruction on the upcoming vocabulary test. I glanced out the window and I couldn't believe what I saw. Dad was on the playground by the kindergarten rooms, pushing my three-year old brother in the swing! They both had smiles on their faces; they looked so happy, so alive. I wanted to run out to greet them, to take my brother in my arms and hug and kiss him, to find out what happened; but I was too timid to ask my teacher if I could leave the room. So I just sat in my wooden desk, gazing through the large, single pane windows, taking mental snapshots of that affectionate moment with great expectancy of what was waiting for me at home.

The fan was on and a piece of green crepe paper from one of our craft activities was stuck in the register and was fluttering freely. The smell of Elmer's paste that we had used earlier still lingered in the room. The noon recess bell rang and the younger kids were going outside for their playtime. Life seemed so right at that moment. Everything felt normal. I watched as Dad and my brother left the playground. They walked away hand in hand. The warmth of that scene filled my whole body with overwhelming joy. We were a family again. I couldn't wait to go home!

At three o'clock, the bell rang I raced through the hallway, being careful not to get caught running so Mrs. Franklin wouldn't scold me. She was the school's portly, mean fourth grade teacher. I was so anxious to see Mom and my little brothers! I ran down the long sidewalk to the street where I could see my house just a block away. Mom's blue station wagon was still parked in the driveway and Dad's white jeep was parked on the grass along the drive. My family was back!

As I got closer to my house, my heart was racing—not because of the rush to get home, but because I was thinking; maybe my Mother just couldn't live without us because she loved us so much, and just maybe she wasn't sick anymore, that her few weeks away had somehow caused her to get well.

Mother was not there. She had dropped off my brother Kevin, who was six years old, at the school earlier that day. She had parked her car in the driveway to leave it and was delivering my brother's clothes when Dad arrived at home after receiving my phone call from the school.

We believe that, if my Dad had not pulled my youngest brother Scott out of Ken's El Camino when he did, Scott would have been gone from our lives forever.

The months and years that followed that bleak day are a complete fog, like a mist rolling in on a cold winter day that consumes the landscape. There is a world out there still very much alive, the sun is shining, life is happening, but the fogginess that hovers over the surface distorts and obscures that part of my life. I have only vague recollections of my now-altered family life from that moment on. I have had to ask my younger brothers what our family was like during those years. Did we play games, did we laugh, what chores did each of us do? I just recently asked my brother Kevin where he and Scott slept after our mother left. I could not visualize their sleeping arrangements. I have struggled to bring to my memory the life that I had during those last years in my home. The emotional distress of Mother deserting me and Father's emotional abandonment was more than a young girl could absorb. It was as if someone had used an eraser and wiped events off the giant white board of my life, leaving only slight traces of red marker imprinted forever in my mind.

Traces Of Red

I did have a few better red-marker moments during those gloomy days. My first kiss has a slight red tinge to it. I will never forget it! It happened during the summer between sixth and seventh grade. I had never even touched a boy's lips before and this first time for me was a very unpleasant experience!

A group of neighborhood kids were congregating around my best friend Kim's house. I had what I thought was a private crush on Tyler; but I must have told Kim, because the next thing I knew, Tyler and I were being pushed around the west corner of the house, behind the overgrown boxwood, and everyone was egging us on. "Kiss, kiss, kiss!" So under the pressure of all the gang, we kissed! Not just a quick smooch on the mouth. Tyler must have been an experienced Romeo, because before I could even protest, I had a wet, slimy tongue in my mouth. I thought I was going to gag and throw up. I remember my head spinning and hearing muffled giggling from the front of the house. I know I blushed because my face was burning hot. Out of embarrassment for not knowing how to kiss and because everyone had watched, I made a mad dash to the comfort of my home and hid in my bedroom, mortified and intrigued all at the same time.

Another moment that is a vague red smear, which cannot be erased, is the ritual of coming home every day after school and making opened-faced peanut butter sandwiches. First, I would slather a large portion of butter on the soft white bread. Then I would put a heaping scoop of creamy peanut butter on top of the butter. My mouth would salivate just waiting to take that first bite. Finally, I would sit down on the blue carpet in front of our black and white television and turn on my favorite afternoon shows, folding my peanut butter sandwich in half and slowly eating that incredibly delicious after school snack.

At 3:30, *Gilligan's Island* was followed by *Lost in Space*, and then, my favorite, *The Brady Bunch*. Something about that family intrigued me. All the activity and comedic chaos was very appealing. They always resolved their problems and that was something I wanted deep within my lonely soul—activity and resolution. What I lived with was silent chaos and no closure to the pain in our lives.

In our house, there would be days when there would literally be no conversation. My brothers and I would silently pass each other in the hallways going to our rooms, the bathroom, or the kitchen. We would make our own meals most of the time, which consisted of cereal by the bowlfuls or TV dinners. Once in a great while I would get the urge to make a pan of brownies or a batch of chocolate chip cookies. The fog of silence and dread filled our home and consumed every cubic inch of it.

As the years passed, the day that I dreaded the most on the calendar was Mother's Day. I could never understand why my brothers' teachers were not more sensitive to our family situation. Every Mother's Day while my younger brothers were attending elementary school, they would come home with their handmade generic gifts for moms. I would mourn another year of not having a Mother to celebrate and honor, but I would also graciously receive the paper plate hearts and construction paper aprons with the words written in little boy handwriting, "Happy Mother's Day," Love Scott and Love Kevin. How I wish I had had the insight to keep those little boy treasures so that they could now share them with their families.

The day that Dad let me have a puppy of my own was a ruby-red joyful day. The runt of her litter, she was a tiny Brittany Spaniel pup! That little friend brought to my life a sense of love and acceptance that a young, broken girl needed so desperately. Instead of a mother waiting at my door after school, I had Cleo. She was all I had, and she was enough to fill the void in my life for a time.

Scarlet smears of pain, red blotches of adolescent discovery, and ruby red marks of joy, I am thankful that I can recall these moments of color in my life.

Blemishes of Youth

As I entered into my adolescence years, I felt a whole new kind of aloneness. No one can prepare you for the onset of womanhood in a home filled with males. I had no one to teach me how to use a sanitary pad, in the days when they had straps and snaps. And later, experimenting with tampons had its interesting moments.

Going bra shopping and talking about boys was not something that I felt I could easily do with Dad, but he was an amazing trooper throughout this chapter in my life. We managed just fine most of the time. He had grown up in a home with no sisters, so these sensitive and personal topics such as menstrual periods and undergarments were never discussed. You can imagine how uncomfortable he must have felt with this role of "only parent," but I am very proud of his efforts. He did the best that he could and we can even laugh about some of it now.

By not having a trusted female in my life during that time to help me through those enormously challenging days, I was headed into a very predictable future. Even if you have a normal, functioning family, the entrance into puberty can be cruel.

I did persevere, but I grew up way too fast and lost the innocence and purity of my childhood as a result of my survival methods. With the absence of a guiding mother and father, I made choices during my adolescent years that would prove to be very damaging to my self-worth. Without going into too much detail, I thought that, in order to get a boy to like me and to keep his affections, all I had to do was "put out" and I would be loved. Of course, as adults, we know that such a pattern does not produce the desired results. Before long I was feeling quite used and abused by all males.

I determined early in my teenage years that high school boys were way too immature, so I turned my interest to the pursuit of older men. Why, I often wondered, did an older man want to date a teenage girl? And why did my Dad not insist that I date boys my own age? Now, as an adult, I understand how the consequences of my choices and the choices of others proved to be so damaging and reinforced untrue and harmful messages in my mind.

This behavior, added to the developing tough-girl image that I proudly paraded around, created inside me a very hard, unfeeling, untrusting, calloused heart. These early trust issues regarding men would follow me for many years. They became the foundation for the walls that I would build to protect myself from more hurt and abandonment by men who got too close to me and to my vulnerable, wounded heart.

Looking back now, I can understand the reasons for my choice of a husband. I naively thought that the man I would choose to marry would be the one who could rescue me from the isolation of my sturdy trust fortifications. This strong fortress would be yet another survival technique that I thought I could master, one that would save me from my fears of rejection, feelings of despair and hopelessness.

I Take This Man

Attending a college out of state was another way I thought I could escape my unpleasant life. I brought to the campus, along with all of my personal belongings, my tough-girl armor that had protected me for so many years. But beneath that hard protective covering was a very shy and insecure girl screaming to be free of the dreadful life that pursued her.

It was in the fall of 1979 when I first caught a glimpse of the attractive young man sitting at one of the long, narrow tables in the campus cafeteria, surrounded by giggling girls. I watched from a distance as this handsome guy skillfully worked his college groupies with humorous stories and Italian-like hand gestures, which resulted in unrestrained laughter from his table guests. I was captivated by this scene and secretly wished that I were one of those girls looking dreamily into this funny man's eyes.

Because of my insecurities, which resulted in my self-protected life, I moved briskly about the campus. I kept my eyes focused forward and never glanced about, in order to give the impression of being self assured and confident. I was completely unaware that the funny man who had intrigued me just days before was also keeping a watchful eye on me as I made my way across the college grounds.

After a couple of flopped dates during my first two weeks at school, I was tempted to surrender to the single life when it happened. The charming stranger that I had secretly watched from afar was in the same lobby where I was using the phone. I had just hung up the phone when I heard this deep, pleasing voice say, "Hello!"

I quickly swung around and there he was, standing right behind me. My heart stopped; I held my breath. *Could I be mistaken? Had this handsome man said that simple word to me, or was he speaking to someone else nearby?*

I looked around, and yes, his greeting was directed at me. I softly replied, "Hello" and shyly bowed my head.

I was not sure what to do next. The air became thick with apprehension. I tried to keep my cool, but palpable bashfulness consumed me and, just as the introductions were about to begin, my date for the evening arrived and stood beside me. I shot a regretful look towards the nameless, handsome man and walked into the waiting room cluttered with older couches and chairs to find my roommate. I started to explain to her that I would not be going out with her because I had a date, but before I could finish my sentence, the familiar pleasant voice broke through my words.

"That's too bad. We were going to have a good time tonight." I was shocked by those words, as was my date. You could feel the testosterone fill the space between the two men and myself. I curiously flashed my eyes towards the appealing voice and yearned for an explanation. I glanced over to my roommate, and all she could do was shrug her shoulders. And with that, my date grabbed my arm, whisked me out of the room, out the wooden double doors and down the concrete steps, getting as far away from the nameless, threatening competitor as he could.

Needless to say, I was now quite intrigued by what had transpired minutes before in the freshman dorm. I was not interested in anything or anyone else for the moment and within an hour or so, I demanded that my date return me to my dorm. Unfortunately it was a Friday night, and I was all alone in my room waiting for hours for my roommate to return. And as I waited, I wondered. *Who was this captivating man and why would he take an interest in me?*

As I paced the tight quarters of my dorm room, I kept an eye on the number tabs that slowly flipped inside my faithful clock. The motor seemed tired from years of use, rotating, minute after minute, grinding and grating as the next number tab dropped. These were the motor-driven timekeepers before the days of digital clocks. In contrast, my mind was spinning rapidly with many questions and dreamy thoughts. The sluggish clicking and flipping was a constant reminder of how dreadfully long this night would be.

Midnight, no roommate. Twelve-thirty, still no sign of her. I knew she would push the limits of the school's weekend curfew as far as she thought she could get away with. The waiting was agonizing. One o'clock, finally I could hear her coming down the hall. I exploded with anticipation as soon as she pushed open the door, "Who is he? What is his name? I am going to marry him!"

Quite taken back by my declaration, she gave me the name that I had so longed to know and my romance with this charismatic man began even before he and I had exchanged another word.

It would be a couple more days before formal introductions were made and within minutes the bond had been set. My heart had not deceived me. I was in love. I knew that this was the man with whom I wanted to spend the rest of my life. Rick was handsome, intelligent, and charming. But it was his wonderful sense of humor that captivated me. It was the one thing that I desperately needed, what I had so long wished for. Laughter and comedic, playful banter, just like the television programs that I had eagerly watched as a little girl. I was spellbound; I had finally found my charming, funny prince who would whisk me away from my unpleasant and lonely life.

After a very short courtship we were engaged. I was thrilled, but needless to say, my father was not. He asked me a couple of times if I was sure this was the man I wanted to marry, and I answered with a heart befuddled by the spell of love, "Yes, Dad, this is the man I want to marry."

Dad accepted my answer, accepted my man and never asked me again. The wedding preparations began.

I truly believed that I was marrying my knight in shining armor, the one who would rescue me and stop the construction of my tall and mighty protective tower. I had formed this conceptual idea that my dream man would create a fairy tale life for me, that he would protect me, love me and cherish me for the rest of our lives ever after. This man that I was choosing to live with for the rest of my life was going to make my life better, he was going to make all of my pain and loneliness go away.

What a feat for anyone to accomplish. I know that my new husband had no idea what he had just signed up for. This would be just one of my many false ideas of what I thought marriage would be like. I did not have any previous example of what a good marriage was, so I became quite skilled in making up my own ideals, however distorted they were.

In my young bride's innocence, I did not realize that my own fractured and damaged past, combined with the traumatic event from my husband's youth and his own abandonment issues, would eventually trigger us into forsaking each other emotionally and physically for years. I now understand the statement that "broken people find broken people." It makes sense. If I had been an emotionally healthy person, I would have chosen an emotionally healthy mate.

Little did I know that this man I fell in love with would be one more person in my life who would create deep wounds of confusion and pain. The catastrophic event that came years later would create such a giant hole in our hearts that only hard work and a miracle of God could heal and mend our wounded and broken souls.

From the very start of being Mr. and Mrs. the ominous clouds of doom began to form. It seemed that I could never outrun the impending storms that continued to invade my life. As the months became years, the flawed ideals that I had so carefully crafted began to fade away into the stark reality of shattered dreams and a broken heart. The romantic notion of a man who would be my noble knight and who would rescue me from the savage beast of loneliness and despair that had pursued me for years could only be found in the fairy tales of my youth. That hot summer day when we looked into each other's eyes and said, "I do" would all too soon be only a wisp of a vapor in our lives.

♥ HEART WORK

Often, we forget to remember how we felt when we first met our spouse. Most of us have never learned how important it is to remember the first time we had loving feelings for him or her. That event launched a sequence of decisions that changed our lives forever. Think about that day. How did you feel? Was it love at first sight, or was it a gradual emotional connection? Were you fearful of falling in love? Were you too trustful? Was your parents' model of marriage ideal? Did you have a false idea of what marriage was supposed to look like, be like?

Most of us had some version of a rescuer in mind when we thought of marriage. Ask yourself the following questions:

What did I think my spouse would do for me?

What needs did I think would be met through marriage?

Did I think my spouse was responsible for how I felt?

Did I believe that my spouse was responsible for my happiness?

Was my spouse supposed to be a reflection of me?

What should my spouse have done to make my life better?

What emotions surface from these thoughts? Write down the feelings that come to mind, the pleasant and the unpleasant.

5

DON'T OPEN THAT DOOR

What is this sadness that we cannot name?

Sarah Ban Breathnach

It wasn't long until some obviously inappropriate behaviors began. I didn't want to see the early signs. They were there, but because of my trust issues and because I had not yet discovered the unknown messages of my childhood, I was too afraid to "open doors." This meant, don't question my husband's behavior.

The first sign was how my husband would subtly flirt with women. He would compliment them right in front of me. I had noticed this behavior while we were dating but dismissed it as innocent conversation. But as it continued into our marriage, inwardly I began to question its meaning. He would be very subtle with his praises, like "You have beautiful eyes" or "You look really nice today." I would always look at him in bewilderment, as if I could not believe my ears, and then shyly I would glance at the women. Sometimes they would stare at me with that look that clearly said, *"Are you going to let him get away with that?"* And at other times it was apparent that they were just as needy of a compliment as I was, and they would totally soak in the pleasure of a man's attention. I never confronted him. My heart would be crushed.

Over the years I would say to myself, *"He is your husband, you can trust him."* I lost track of how many times I gave myself that little pep talk. I would reprimand myself, dismiss the subtle signs and chalk it up to my own struggle with insecurities.

Tattered Treasures

Just as I had thought that marrying my prince would save me from my past, I convinced myself that, if only I was a mother, then I could survive this unfortunate life of loneliness and despair. To bring children into my chaos was one of my greatest fears, and yet the desire to become a mother was very powerful. I yearned to share the abundance of love that was stored up within me. I made a vow with myself when I was a young woman that I would be the best mother in the world, that I would make up for the years that I had lost as a child, that I would pour all that I had within me into loving my own children.

I am so very thankful to God that I had the opportunity to fulfill that desire. The day that each one of my boys was born will forever be cherished in my heart.

I delivered our first son when, after twenty-three grueling hours of labor with only nurses monitoring my progress, there seemed to be a problem. The delivery doctor finally arrived and said frantically, "Get this baby out now!" Since this was my first delivery I did not know what to expect, so I was a bit shocked by the doctor's reaction.

Competent nurses followed the doctor's bellowed orders and within minutes I was rushed into the delivery room. A team of doctors and nurses quickly prepped me for a vaginal delivery. As the gowns and gloves were rapidly put on, we were informed that the umbilical cord was wrapped so tightly around my baby's neck that with each contraction and subsequent push I had been unknowingly strangling my baby over and over again. The labor had gone on too long and my baby's head was too far down the birth canal, so an emergency C-section was out of the question. So was the option of an epidural drip. I would have to endure what was to come on my own, without the help of pain relieving medications.

Controlled confusion was everywhere, the scent of a sterilizing agent filled the room, overhead lights were dimmed, medical instruments clinked and clanged as the medical team gathered the needed supplies, and the constant beeping of the fetal monitor chimed in my head. I was frightened and exhausted, constantly concerned about the welfare of our child.

With stirrups positioned, legs spread apart, oxygen mask placed over my mouth and nose, I earnestly looked into my husband's eyes. I saw only distress reflecting back. So much was happening so fast, my mind was spinning. *"Was my baby going to live?"* I moaned deeply as the doctor placed both of his hands inside the birth canal and grasped my baby's head, skillfully severing the lifeline between my unborn child and me. He quickly, proficiently pulled our baby out.

I will never forget the fear that gripped my husband and me as the concerned doctor tenderly held our son in his capable, strong hands and repetitively chanted, "Breathe, baby, breathe," as if he were begging some unknown force in the room to release the death grip on our child's lungs. My husband and I both held our breath, desperately waiting for our firstborn son to breathe in his first. After what seemed forever, our sweet little boy took his first life-giving breath. Tears of relief erupted from me. We could breathe at last; our little boy had won his battle between life and death. I have often wondered since that day, *Did God give my son the same will to survive? Was he, too, a fighter?*

I can vividly recall how our newborn son snuggled quietly in my arms. He fit so perfectly, like the final piece of a great, big laborious puzzle was in place. I was complete. As he suckled on my swollen breasts, I pondered over the events of the last several hours. I lovingly gazed upon my sleeping child and I thanked God over and over for sparing my son; he was perfect, and he was healthy.

I was a mother. I had dreamed of this day since I was a child, and now here I was, a young woman with a purpose. Now my life would make sense. I had so much love to give.

Five years later, we now had three beautiful boys. What a blessing they were, but they did not come without many challenges. As any mother who has raised children knows, breast-feeding while the other little ones demand your attention, two in diapers and mounds of laundry, the jealous antics of older siblings, and the many sleepless nights of colicky tantrums can be very trying. But, oh, the joy of having children to love, to care for, and to distract me from the shattered dreams of what I thought a marriage was suppose to be.

I recently pulled out my collection of photo albums. My family's story is told throughout those worn pages. As I opened each album and turned each page, the memories flooded back and nurtured my soul.

I treasure those memories and, with the passing of each year, I have longed for the chance to embrace each one of my little boys just one more time. If only I could remember the scent of their sweet baby breath. How I wish I could capture the moment and never let go the memory of the first time their tender, little voices whispered "Mommy, I love you" in my ear and ended the loving gesture with a gentle, wet kiss on my lips. I wish that I could have saved every one of the dandelion bouquets that they spontaneously gathered for me. I would have lingered longer as nasty bugs and slimy pollywogs enraptured my little boys. I would have tried harder to learn how to make more realistic car sounds, and I would have been more at ease with kissing wounded dinosaur boo-boo's away. If I could do it over again, I would let my little darlings stomp in more mud puddles; I would not be so picky about what foods I felt they needed to eat; I would read an extra bedtime story; and I would not fuss so much over their clothes and hair.

I truly treasure each memory that I have so richly and abundantly received by giving birth to three rambunctious, sweet, wonderful boys. Oh, the blessings of motherhood; I am forever thankful.

As I reassembled some of the photos that had become unstuck and shifted from the album page, I gently grasped the memory of that day in my fingers and tried to relive the feelings and the place and time each photo recorded. Then, very carefully, as if I was handling a very fragile, valuable piece of art, I placed the colorful treasure back in the empty space reserved for the escaped snapshot, secured once again with clear adhesive tape so the sequence of the events could be preserved for a lifetime.

As the years have passed, those tattered collections of memories and photos are a balm to my heart. They bring back the joy that at times seemed to have gotten lost as I dealt with the heartache of broken dreams and shattered hopes.

Passages

The early days of childrearing would prove to be life changing and challenging but nothing compared to what was to come. I often wondered as I journeyed through this passage of time what I had done wrong in my life to deserve such pain and heartache. I must have angered God in some way. Why did life have to inflict such pain?

For some mysterious reason, the constant and unmerciful assaults of the devastating beast of gloom and despair that had pursued me for years were determined to stalk my young family as well. But now, I had three little boys to protect and to defend. I was determined to survive, I would survive—my family depended on it.

For ten years, one hectic moment would lead to another equally- challenging moment. My oldest son Caleb was six years old when he was diagnosed with ADD (attention deficit disorder). He struggled all throughout his school years, but not only in his studies. Caleb was also severely and repeatedly teased and bullied by his peers. Caleb's teachers seemed unable or unwilling to recognize his unique learning style, which was quite different from the mainstream boys and girls in his classes. The teachers created an atmosphere that proved to be detrimental. By the time Caleb was sixteen years old, he gave up trying to satisfy his teachers. When he could not take the cruel abuse of his peers any longer, he dropped out of school.

The hours and hours that went into creating rewards for progress and incentives for not giving up became overwhelming at times. No systems, no amount of goal setting, no incentive regimen seemed to help this struggling young boy. As a mother, I would agonize over why I could not help him be successful with his social and study skills. Just prior to his early exit from high school, Caleb began regularly spending time with a group of kids that accepted him the way he was. He fit into their standards of living. These broken and lost teens felt they were the misfits of this world. As a result, his choice of friends and activities carried him far, far away from the safety of our home. Over the next several years Caleb would live on the streets or in drug houses, become addicted to meth, pop acid, and deaden his emotional pain by smoking mind-numbing marijuana. For many months I languished under the unrelenting weight and unbearable anguish of the unknown. Was my son dead or alive?

My second son Luke was born with a lung disorder that caused him to suffer with severe croup. I remember the many nights we spent sitting together, either in a steamy bathroom or bundled up in blankets on the front porch in the humid early morning hours. I would coach him on how to take deep breaths, one after another, to help calm the swelling in his lungs.

One summer, my husband and I had gone out of town and left each of the boys with a different family. To ask anyone to take care of all three boys was to risk strained relationships when we returned; they were quite a handful, to put it mildly.

While we were gone, Luke, twelve at the time, had a terrible episode of what was later diagnosed as asthma. He had to be rushed to the hospital in an ambulance all by himself. Luke was frightened to be all alone. The fear he had experienced during a previous summer, when he was lost and separated from our family in an amusement park, came flooding back and only added to his terror. Because he could not breathe, Luke truly believed that he was dying; and because we were not with him during that harrowing event, he was traumatized, resulting in reoccurring panic attacks and severe depression. These health disorders would affect his friendships, his schoolwork and every aspect of his life. There were days when Luke was too frightened to go to school; he could not shake the reoccurring thoughts of death and he did not want to be away from me when it happened. He lived with so much fear surrounding his breathing issues. It would take years and more patience than I thought I had to help him through those difficult days. Luke would literally be paralyzed with his afflictions.

My third son Jacob was also diagnosed with ADHD (attention deficit hyperactive disorder), emphasis on the hyperactive! His compulsive behavior would create profound fear in me. At times I felt this son would be the one that could possibly bring me down. I was not sure if I would survive this youngest son's constant activity and at times dangerous behaviors. Jacob's little body had so much energy that I could hardly keep up. I could write a book about all the amazingly ingenious displays of mischievous and cunning antics that he pulled, and I probably don't even know the half of them! Before Jacob was finished with his middle-school years, he had been in trouble with the law a couple of times and just barely escaped spending time in the juvenile detention system.

While the boys were each growing up in their individual ways, I suffered with fibromyalgia, a chronic pain syndrome that pushed my body and mind to the extreme. For ten years I battled acute pain and fatigue; I could find no relief. Not a position or a painkiller would lessen the excruciating and debilitating pain. And if that in itself was not enough, I would also on a monthly basis deal with chronic yeast infections and vaginal sores that would have me literally screaming when I urinated or had a bowel movement.

I was not one who would have ever considered suicide. But there comes a time when you reach the point where you think you cannot survive one more day.

I was suffering. Night after night, I would not sleep. In the morning, I would drag myself out of bed, stand underneath a hot shower and pray that I could muster up enough will power and strength to make it through another day.

I felt as if I had literally been run over by a truck. The pain that ravaged my body was intolerable. It felt like someone was stabbing me with hot daggers dipped in poison, then twisting and turning them deep into my hips and back. The burning sensation never seemed to subside. It penetrated deep within my muscle tissues and nerves. I could not lie on one side for more than a couple of minutes without fiery pain, which resulted in tossing and turning all through the night.

Day after day, I stood under a hot, steaming shower to caress my sore and weary body. I would then begin the long, draining task of getting three boys off to school on time, before going to work myself (I was a Special Ed. Assistant, working with severely disabled students).

After work I would come home, be a mom, help with homework, fix dinner maybe, do laundry, and then face the difficult task of putting three overly active boys to bed. At the end of the day, the last thing I wanted was to have sex. Because of the yeast infections and vaginal sores, sex was out of the question during at least two or three weeks of the month. What I wanted was to be held, to be told that I could hang in there. I longed to hear Rick say, *"I know you're exhausted; how about tomorrow I do the laundry, or wash the dishes?"* I would have loved to have had help putting the boys to bed.

The guilt that I carried of not being able to be a good mother and not being a desirable wife lay heavy on my heart. I would suffer silently. I never once complained out loud. But like I said, you can only take so much.

Enough!

I clearly remember the day. I was driving down a busy highway on a blustery, wet fall morning. I had just dropped off my youngest son at his elementary school and was on my way to work when my mind started to wander. I reminded myself of how dreadful I felt that my life was. My boys were at times so difficult to handle, my husband was way too occupied with the ministry, and the torturous physical pain that I carried with me had taken its toll. That's when I saw the perfect solution; I had a plan. About a half a mile away, coming rapidly towards me, was a semi tractor-trailer hauling a full load of fresh-cut timbers. I thought to myself, *"This is it. It could be over in just a few seconds!"* I grasped the steering wheel with both hands to steady myself, and as the weight-burdened truck drew closer and closer, I saw myself go through with it.

In the mere seconds that it took, I envisioned in my mind's eye what my family would be saying at my funeral. I saw the anguish on my boy's faces. But in that moment, as I strained to peer through the blurred windshield, my mind numbed by the rhythmic beat of the heavy raindrops, I began to question myself. *"Why? Why did my husband show no emotion, no tears, no sorrow. How could he just apathetically stand by my casket and not weep? Didn't we love each other? Didn't my life matter to him? Did my life matter to me?"*

The semi truck passed. I turned up the pace of my windshield wipers to wipe away the deluge of water that the sixteen-wheeler had sprayed onto my car. I wished that it could be just as simple to erase the longing in my heart for a life that did not cause so much heartache. I loosened my death grip on the steering wheel; my heart rate began to return to normal. I felt such sorrow and hopelessness. I felt like such a failure. I couldn't even bring myself to end this pain and misery.

In reality I did not want to die. I wanted to live. I wanted a life filled with happiness and joy. I wanted a husband who truly loved me, one who would cherish me, even if in the future this debilitating syndrome that plagued my body landed me in a wheelchair. I so desperately wanted my boys to care about their lives like I did.

I never again had thoughts of ending it all.

You don't get to choose how you're going to die. Or when.
You can only decide how you're going to live. Now.

Joan Baez

♥ HEART WORK

Think about your life as a married couple. Were there any red flags that indicated there was a problem in your relationship? If you did notice them, what were they? How do you feel, knowing the signs were there but (possibly out of fear) they were pushed into denial? Perhaps there were no signs at all and you were completely taken by surprise. How does this make you feel?

Sometimes, we get so busy with the chaos of life that we don't think about the precious moments in our lives. If you have children, ponder their lives for a few minutes. Write down some of your most endearing memories regarding each child. Those memories can be quite soothing during these difficult days. Someday, be willing to share your writings with them; your children will be delighted to hear about the silly antics or sweet affections they displayed.

In your past, have you ever felt like giving up? Perhaps you did not want to end your life, but did you think that, if you walked away from the stress and difficulties of your life, the issues would be resolved? How do you feel right now? Do you feel like giving up? Do you feel like walking away from it all—the job, the family, the marriage? Go back to the Appendix and read over the list of feeling words and write down several words that trigger a feeling or thought. With as much detail as you can, write about what each word has provoked in you.

6

Behind Closed Doors

If a home doesn't make sense, nothing does.

Henrietta Ripperger

Many years ago, my husband was a minister of a thriving church. I will never forget the day when he came home from a very exhausting day of work and told me, "I am going to sacrifice you and the boys for the church."

I stood there dumbfounded and thought to myself, *"How do you compete with a man of God? He must know what he is doing."* And once again, fearing to open a door by asking a question, I said nothing.

I would be perplexed and hurt, wondering how my husband could stand in front of a large congregation week after week and preach the most life-changing and challenging messages about "How to Have a Great Marriage," "Will the Family Survive?" and "Secrets of Deep Relationships," to name just a few. He would counsel couples about their failing marriages. They would do the hard work and their marriages seemed to flourish. I would wonder: Why couldn't we have an endearing love relationship? Why couldn't we live behind closed doors the way that we pretended in public, the way he preached that families should be?

Secluded in our bedroom we would have the same arguments over and over. After much bantering back and forth, the problem with our marriage was always me; I didn't try hard enough and I didn't want sex enough. I had "issues" that I needed to work on. I cared more for the kids than for him. And I would always get defensive and put up my protective walls. I would tell him to stop talking down to me; I would complain that he treated me like his child, not his wife. He would get angry and usually walk out of the room. In any conversation regarding counseling, he would tell me that I was the one "messed up" and that I "needed to go get well." We blamed each other, we denied our faults, and out of self-protection, we withheld our affections.

My husband and I succumbed to the strain of our marital brokenness. We learned to veil the pain and impending doom by distracting ourselves with what looked like healthy behaviors. We harvested the unwanted consequences of this kind of marriage: isolation and resulting aloneness.

Diversions

Your spouse may not be a minister of a church, but if you are reading this, you may know something of the pain of aloneness that I am talking about. Businesses that consume, employers that are demanding, schedules that dictate lives or hobbies often rob intimacy. The effects of these priorities batter the homes of men and women who sacrifice their families. In many cases they are driven to work-a-holism as a .

means of medicating their accumulated emotional pain. For some of you, your spouse may have no motivation whatsoever to contribute to the household finances or obligations. Computer use, video gaming or excessive television viewing can be forms of distraction that rob intimacies. The results can cause devastating destruction to marriages and families. Self-pity often covers the personal sense of shame or guilt from past personal traumas. In reality, it is most often their own brokenness and insecurity that drive them; they just have not yet discovered the wounds that formed their dysfunctional choices.

My children became my diversion. I was determined to become the best mother in the whole world. I would be the mother to my boys that I never had. I would overcompensate for their absent father. I would be one-hundred-percent present with them and nothing would interfere. I over protected them, over indulged them to medicate my pain of marital dysfunction and buried childhood wounds. All the while I was subconsciously protecting myself from the pain of my broken marriage. My emotional protective walls were becoming very tall and extremely resilient in order to hide my loneliness and heartbreak. Unfortunately, I had no idea how damaging those walls would be. Those enormous fortifications that I had built around my heart were not protecting me. In reality, they were creating a thicker and thicker wall of strong emotional mortar and rock between me and my husband and my children. I was trying to protect my heart from more heartache and disappointment, but by doing so, I created more pain for myself.

In my early isolation days, the all-consuming emptiness of aloneness became such a part of me that I didn't know any other way of life. "*This is it, deal with it,*" would be a frequent prompt I gave myself. Then it happened. One hot summer afternoon, I did not have the capacity to deal with it any longer. With my three boys playing outside, I locked myself in the bathroom, mechanically undressing, pulling back the plastic shower curtain, turning on the water and standing beneath the pulsating spray. For me it took that crazy act of taking a warm shower in the middle of the day, for no other reason than a hope that the sound of running water would drown out the uncontrollable tears and sobs of despair. I needed to finally bring myself to the realization that my life was totally messed up. It was a pitiful act, for sure, but one that proved to be quite beneficial to my future and my life.

Once again I embraced my survival instincts, pulled myself together and became more determined than ever before never to give up on my pursuit of the life that I desired. I did the only thing that I could think of to do, the only thing that I found that would give me some relief. I poured myself into a relationship with the only one who I felt might understand me: God. And I made another appointment with my counselor.

The Apathetic Heart

> We believe that there are only two kinds of marriages,
> the good and bad
> but really there are three—good, bad, and indifferent.
> And the last of the three is really the worst kind.
>
> Sarah Ban Breathnach

Indifference means that there is a tendency for a person to be detached or unfeeling when a display of interest or affection would be in order. I would have to agree with Sarah Ban Breathnach, this is the worst kind of marriage, and this is the kind of marriage that we had. An indifferent marriage will literally destroy you as a couple and as individuals. I remember when indifference reared its ugly head. I didn't realize how damaging it was until it was too late.

This display of detachment made its grand appearance during a period of two weeks when a friend of ours came to visit. A few months prior she had lost her husband to cancer and she was in need of some time to get away and recover from the stress that comes of losing a loved one. We invited her to come to our home to rest, relax by the pool and take mini day trips hiking in the mountains that were close to the little community where we lived.

Throughout her visit, my husband and I would have these little spats. It was quite obvious that we did not like each other at times, which in a healthy relationship can happen, but you work through those difficult times and grow together. In the past, however, I would never have allowed quarreling to be out in the open for all to see. I would always stuff my feelings and frustrations under my emotional rug. But for some reason it was spilling out, so our friend was quite aware of our relational conflicts.

Over the course of our friend's visit, I began to notice that my husband would treat her with care and respect, while being utterly rude to me. It felt like she was his wife and I was the housekeeper and the cook. When I finally could not take the ill treatment any longer, I asked him why he would disrespect me and treat her with so much compassion and kindness. His response? He felt sorry for her because she didn't have a husband anymore and he wanted her to have a nice time while she was in our home. Because of my good heart I backed down, but instinctive awareness began invading my mind. I had become very good at disregarding the flags that regularly slapped my face and heart, and I would automatically force the thoughts away. Remember? I didn't want to open those doors and face the trouble.

In the middle of her visit, my husband had been asked to speak at a high school summer camp in central Idaho. She happily volunteered to stay in our home for a couple of days while we were gone and take care of our dogs and keep an eye on our youngest son for us.

The day that he was to speak just happened to be our twenty-first wedding anniversary. I was looking forward to a break from all of the chaos and was hoping that we could spend some romantic time together, something that was lacking in our lives. We drove two hours to get to the camp, then my husband spoke to the kids and, by the time we reached our lodging, it was after midnight. We were both tired, but he needed to unwind from the busy day. He wanted to watch a movie, but the only TV was in the master bedroom. I was frustrated. I did not want to waste two more hours; I wanted to connect on a deeper level. But instead of putting up a fuss and ruining a good night of rest, I crossed the hallway to the guest bedroom and, after much isolated thinking in my head, wishing that things could be different, I fell asleep, alone, in a strange bed. It was not a great way to spend our wedding anniversary.

Indifference had crept in and we had succumbed to its numbing effect. Our relationship had become so unexciting and dull, that even going to a romantic log cabin in the mountains couldn't ignite our extinguished love.

Returning home from our unromantic get-away, we had one day left before our friend's departure and that last twenty-four hours would prove to be the loneliest and the most confusing hours of my married life.

We had decided to take our guest to a rodeo. She had never been to one before, and we thought it would be fun to expose her to a little bit of the authentic Idaho country life. We had been invited to have dinner before the rodeo with a few of my husband's horse buddies at a local Mexican restaurant. After we had chosen our seats around the long oblong table, the introductions were made. When he introduced our friend, he told the guys, "And this is my best friend." Stunned, I looked across the table and stared at her beaming face. The introductions were over. My husband had forgotten to introduce me. You'd have to be a stupid idiot not to pay attention to the red banners that were flapping in my face. I sat there furious. How dare he introduce everyone but me! But more than that, I burned inside; I could hear his words repeated, over and over, *my best friend.* I lost my appetite and pushed my enchilada around my plate with my fork and didn't say a word throughout the rest of the mealtime.

After dinner we made our way to the rodeo. There had been some kind of mix up with the tickets and we could not all sit together, so we had to split up. After a minute of uncomfortable discussions about who would sit where, I furiously took two tickets, one for myself and one for my youngest son, and we sat on the opposite side of the large stadium. We found ourselves sitting directly across from my husband, his "best friend," and all the rest of his buddies. What torture, what heartache. I don't recall watching the rodeo at all. My mind was racing. I was angry, confused, and emotionally exhausted. I stared across the dusty arena at the two of them having a good time together, smiling at each other and pointing at the competitors; they were completely unaware of my fixed gaze. As the cowboys and their trusty animal companions won their awards, I was losing my man. Slowly and painfully he was slipping away.

The next day was Sunday and after the church services I nervously asked my husband to come into our bedroom; I needed to talk to him. We sat down together on our king-sized bed and, with much fear of what the outcome of this conversation would be, I came right out and asked him, "Are you sexually attracted to her?"

His response was immediate. "No, no way!" Then I asked; "Are you emotionally attracted to her?"

He hesitated, and then reluctantly said, "Yes." He then began to try explaining to me that she understood him and that she was like a best friend. He told me that she was very wise and gave him godly counsel. I told him that he was walking in dangerous territory and that he needed to get help, we needed help. He said he was fine, he could handle it. I tried to push it more, but to no avail. The conversation ended. I was not satisfied, but I felt as if I had better move away from the topic. I had dared to open the door just a crack, but my fear would not allow me to push it any further. I was so thankful she was leaving that afternoon.

Later that week, I received a letter from this friend. She told me that she loved my husband and that she would always love him, no matter what I thought. They were always going to be good friends. She continued to stab my heart with jabbing statements—she thought he was the most amazing pastor she had ever known and that, while she was visiting with us, she had noticed how badly I had treated him and that he deserved better. And then, as if the pain of her bitter words were not enough to bear, she thrust the knife deeper into my already bleeding soul and lectured me on how messed up I was and that I had better seek more counseling to figure out why I didn't like having women for friends. She told me that I had some very deep issues and she was pretty sure that my mother had something to do with it. She then said that our marriage was in trouble and that obviously my husband was not satisfied with me as a wife. In closing she said that she knew that this letter would probably destroy our friendship, but she was okay with that as long as I got some help.

I was distraught, I was terrified, and I felt very betrayed. She was my friend. How could she have been so cruel and so distorted in her accusations? We had had a few conversations over the last months prior to her visit regarding how I was trying really hard to work on my marriage, how I wanted to be a better wife. I had chosen to be vulnerable with her about my private life and now this! I couldn't believe what I had just read.

Confused, I sat alone in my quiet house and wept. My world was spiraling out of control. What was happening? I could feel in my heart that something was not right. But I couldn't or wouldn't allow myself to trust my intuitions. So much of my life had been about not trusting myself. I felt my soul was hemorrhaging. Silently and violently, my inner self was dying.

It's like a bruise. A powerful strike causes the blue and black to appear, but underneath the surface the damage has been done. The bruise is a warning that something is wounded at a deeper level. I was wounded and the black and blue discoloration was just beginning to become very apparent.

After so many attempts to believe in what I thought was true and then to be shamed or told that I am the one messed up, I began to agree. I would tell myself that what I was thinking was just crazy—that I needed to trust my husband. After all, he is a minister.

Later that day I waited anxiously for my husband to come home from the office. I watched through the front window as he pulled into the driveway. I could hear his keys rattling as he locked the car. He walked through the garage entrance; it shut automatically behind him with a subtle click. He then went straight to our bedroom and turned on the TV. I followed him and sat down on our bed facing him. Anxiously I fixed my eyes on him, told him about the letter and then decided to read it out loud to him. His response? "It's about time someone told you the truth."

He then continued watching the evening news. I asked what he meant by that and he proceeded to tell me again, rather annoyed this time, that I had some major issues to deal with and that I should listen to my friend's advice and get help.

My husband's cutting words would linger in my memory for many months. My soul had been crushed, not because of the usual *"You go get help"* messages. I was almost numb to those. But it was his response to the letter: *"It's about time someone told you the truth."* He didn't even defend me when she wrote, "Obviously he is not satisfied with you as a wife." Those words were the most difficult to read.

The grief that came over me was unbearable. I felt that, not only was I losing my husband, but also that I must be losing my mind. I was angry with this "friend," for her words cut deep into my soul.

I had had so many hours of counseling, but at this moment in time it felt as if I had wasted my money and my time. For years I had taken the blame for our broken relationship and here once again, I was the problem, I was the messed up one and now my husband had a collaborating friend who agreed with him.

I didn't even know how to respond. I wanted to ask "the question," the one that I had wanted to ask for so many long months: "Are you having an affair?" But how could I? I was the obvious problem in this relationship.

It was as if I had been given a dose of poison. The first swallow of reality was quite bitter, and then the slow agonizing death would follow. A part of me died that day and every day that followed; the poisonous venom of indifference would destroy any hopes of a marriage that I had always dreamed of.

I share that painful and embarrassing part of my story to let you know that I had yet another decision to make after that painful period of poisonous indifference. I could either be consumed by my broken, dysfunctional life and let the effects of those circumstances atrophy what was left of my emotional well-being, or I could choose to do everything in my power to fight for what I wanted in my life.

Where Is My Prince?

For twenty-one years I had tried every tactic that I thought would work to make my husband love me. But all of my strategic planning had failed. Instead I became more isolated, more alone, desperate and extremely emotionally fatigued.

The only way that I had survived the emotional pain of my broken life was by shielding myself from the despair of my messed up relationship. The consequences of false messages that ravaged my mind, and the resulting brokenness that it created early in my life, drove me to continue to build strong and mighty walls around my heart. Ascending into my protective tower, I watched my world fall apart. I confined myself to this fortress of seclusion and suffered with depression, aloneness, and, oh, so much confusion.

Behind these fortified walls, I camouflaged my isolation with many distractions. Oh, the distractions seemed healthy enough: my children, my career, and community activities. I even medicated my pain with what could be called innocent vices. I read novels that would help me escape into a fantasy world. I spent hours and hours designing and tending to my garden. The television or computer became a constant companion. Many other distractions medicated my pain. Retail therapy, social events, or eating certain comfort foods would within minutes change the chemicals in my body and help mask the difficult events of the day.

That is what is so dangerous about these behaviors. They looked so normal, they felt so right, and I was really good at convincing myself they were. To see me in public, no one would think that inside my head and behind closed doors my life was just one big, disordered, dysfunctional mess.

All of these "harmless" behaviors created such a dilemma. My coping methods became ordinary routines and, as life continued to plunge more and more out of control, my mental and emotional fortress got stronger, the walls got thicker, and the more fortified my heart became. The diversions kept my crazy feelings at bay and the vicious cycle was repeated over and over.

These seemly safe diversions became destructive and toxic to me and to the lives of my sons whom I was trying to protect. My children were affected by the dysfunction that went on within the four walls of our home. Their lives were reflecting what was really going on behind closed doors.

Even as I tried to hide the effects of my tormented relationship with their dad from my children, it seeped out like toxic fumes that over time caused great damage to their surrounding environment. How could it not? Our boys absorbed the poison of indifference, anger, selfishness, and relational disrepair. I have often wondered why our oldest son Caleb would choose to destroy his life with such harmful devices. Maybe the pain he was trying to numb was the toxicity of his youth in a home built on pretense. What was shown to the outside world was not the true story of what was really happening inside.

The effects of such conditions in our home influenced the way each of our boys viewed their lives, and the consequences of their behaviors would follow them into their futures. I had to decide, was I going stay in my tower or was I bravely going to tear down my protective fortress? I knew that with either choice my family would be significantly affected. The first option would allow the dysfunction to continue, and without a doubt the poison of indifference and consequential emotional damage would pass down through to the next generation and beyond. It had already begun; the obvious cost of our sons' choices was destroying any chance that they might live somewhat normal lives. The other alternative could shatter the opposing wall of broken-ness and create a new future for my family and myself. With or without my Prince Charming, I would find my way out of my fortified tower. I was determined never to give up on the life that I had so long desired.

The Demolition Begins

I began to initiate the dismantling of my stronghold, one burdensome boulder at a time. I began removing the false messages of my youth. I felt as if I were on some archaeo-logical dig. Shoveling and hauling out the unwanted debris, then carefully excavating artifacts of historical importance. The work was exhausting and overwhelming at times; sweat and tears would be constant companions. As the worked progressed I began to see results. The thick, strong fortress that surrounded my heart and life was being torn down. If I did not focus on doing this for me, then I knew that I would never live the life that I had so desperately wanted, the life that I believed could be possible. I began the demoli-tion of my secure and safe fortress.

The sessions with my therapist were difficult, but it was even more challenging to practice what I was trying to learn. Over time I began to uncover the unfortunate mes-sages from my childhood, and during the dismantling of my protective walls, I would pray. I prayed for a miracle. The arrival of that miracle seemed to be uncertain. Would I live the rest of my life in a solitary marriage? I was determined to fight; I would continue to battle the destroying beast of hopelessness and despair. I would not allow it to torment my life and marriage forever. I would not.

Some women wait for something to change
and nothing does change
so they change themselves.

Audre Lord

♥ HEART WORK

"The opposite of relational disrepair is intimacy"

What happened behind the closed doors in your home? During arguments, did you blame each other for the brokenness in your relationship? Out of self-protection, did you or your spouse withhold affection—knowingly or unknowingly? Were you able to share honestly your deep feelings and desires with your spouse? If not, what do you think the reasons were? What are some of the diversions you used to help you cope with stress?

Did apathy creep in and rob your relationship of intimacies long ago? In your journal, write a list of all the times in your life when indifference showed up. (Remember, indifference means lack of interest, lack of enthusiasm or being dispassionate when a display of interest or affection would be in order.) Create a column for you and one for your spouse. (The one for your spouse is there for you to put those thoughts down so they won't get in the way.) Your column will be where you will want to spend your time and energy.

Once you feel the list is complete, write a description of what a preferred future would look like for each item on the list. Dare to dream here—it's time to start recovering you.

How had you settled in your relationship with your spouse? What part of you did you give up? What version of you did you set out to be when you first met, and how have you changed? Write down what did not work in your relationship and why, and the feelings that arise as a result. As you write this narrative, it is likely that more strong emotions will emerge. THIS IS A GOOD THING. It will not feel good; it's quite possible that you have not located these feelings before, but they are very important.

7

LOVE FORSAKEN

How long will you forget me? Forever?
How long will you hide from me?
How long must I worry and feel sad in my heart all day?
Answer me, my God; tell me ...

Psalm 13:1-3, New Century Version

The days passed by like rolling thunderclouds, at times filled with such dreary doom. My children continued to live out their lives in ways that repeatedly broke my heart. I would persistently cry out to God, *"Why, why does it have to be so hard?"* And with silent remorse I would say, *"I don't want to live this life anymore."* But as I had always done before, I picked myself up from the dusty ground one more time and continued the fight.

So I struggled on. I continued with my therapy. I consistently tried to love my boys unconditionally, and I would pray daily for a miracle in my marriage. I felt myself getting stronger. I knew I was getting emotionally well, but it was slow progress. The uphill battles would rage. Every once in awhile I would find myself sitting comfortably on top of a captured emotional rampart like a weary warrior finding temporary reprieve from a recent crusade. My life would occasionally be calm for a short season. It was as if I was gazing upon rich green meadows of wild flowers, the sweet scent of honey clover lingering in the crisp evening air. I could soak in the pleasure of colorful sunsets and relax under the sparkling stars overhead. Yes, I would have moments like that, and when they occurred I would cherish them. A very wise friend told me that those days had to exist or my life would have imploded. I believe she was right. So when those days came about, I would enjoy the peace for a time, knowing that the next day could bring with it brutal darkness and gloom from yet another relational conflict.

During the days and months that followed that bleak summer afternoon when I received the betraying letter of a friend and the shattering words of my husband's response, the only survival technique that that seemed to work for me was to pray daily for my family. Tucked inside the pages of my Bible I carefully stored the one and only current family photo that I had. It had been taken on the previous Christmas when we were fortunate to get all three boys home together. It is such a sad thought to me that during those tumultuous years we only got together as a family once or twice a year. If we were fortunate, our oldest son would reappear from the death clutch of the streets around the holidays and we would act as if we were one happy family. So on this one particular Christmas day, before my son would be robbed from my life once again for months on end, I seized the moment for a photo op. I am so very thankful that I did, for it would be a two more years before the next opportunity would arise to have my family together again.

The Final Strike

One year, two months and three days after that August nightmare terrorized my sleep, my husband confessed his unfaithfulness. The destroying beast had made its final strike. I was done with the marriage. I was justified. I had perfect and righteous reasons to file for divorce. I was not going to stay with a man who deliberately chose to live with his deceitful lies, while at the same time emotionally abusing me for years with accusations that I was the one in our relationship that was messed up and needed to get help. I was astounded by the fact that he could numbly confess his infidelity and shed no tears or show any sorrow for his betrayal. I knew in my heart that he must not be truly sorry for the devastation that he had brought into our home. With tormented emotional agony that lasted throughout that darkest of all nights, I painstakingly wrestled for hours trying to decide what I would do the following day. Would I leave my husband of twenty-two years? What was I going to tell our boys? What would I do with my dog and my belongings? I would vacillate with my thoughts until I could bear it no more and then uncontrollable sobbing would follow. This ritual of planning my departure and irrepressible weeping would be repeated over and over, as if I was on some wacky amusement park ride and the mechanical parts had been broken. There was no escaping the cruel torment.

I became a prisoner in my own guest bedroom, not daring to leave its confining four walls and step out into the reality of my now shattered, dismantled life. I could not sleep, I could not pray, I could not think clearly. Inhaling and exhaling became laborious as inconsolable grief complicated my ability to breathe. I could not grasp what had just happened to my life. All those years of refusing to "open those doors" to ask questions or to confront issues, and now here I was, bound with the chains of despair and living with the stark reality that my dreaded nightmare had come to pass. The horrid creature's claws of my dream had ripped my heart into shreds, blood gushed from the inflicted wound. I held my hands over my breast trying to breathe, trying to make sense of this mess. How could this have happened to me?

All night I was desperately trying to plan my next move. When I could not tolerate the isolated pain any longer, I called a close friend at 2:00 A.M. and shared with her how my life had just blown apart. She consoled me, she cried with me, she loved me and out of her generous heart she offered the guest suite in her home as a place of refuge and I accepted. I would be there that following night.

The plan was set. I would get up first thing in the morning and leave this protective shell of a room, ask my boys what they wanted to do, stay with their father or go with me back to Washington state and take up residence with my dear friend Deana. The rest of the details I did not have; I just knew that I was no longer going to be in the same house with an unfaithful, deceiving man. I had it all worked out.

Finding no comfortable position I sat up in bed and wrapped my arms tightly around my knees, holding them deeply to my chest. As I continued struggling to breathe, something profound happened that changed my world forever.

As I waited for the darkness of night to end, my heart and mind hemorrhaging with dread and fear. I felt like I was reliving the nightmare that had invaded my dreams so many months before. As I wrestled and screamed at the destroying beast, "No, this is not happening to me! No, this cannot possibly be happening to me!" something so otherworldly, so surreal happened. In that moment, in the midst of my despairing cries, I heard a very faint voice, both soft and commanding at the same time. How could that be? How could I hear anything at all? But it *was* a voice. Was it audible? I do not know, but what I do know is the dialogue between the gentle but firm voice and myself was very clear and direct.

The instruction was this: "*You do not abandon little boys; you love them, you hold them. You do not leave them.*" I struggled for a moment with those words. Had I heard right? I wanted to make them mean that I was not to leave my two sons with their father. But I knew, somehow, that was not what was meant. In my heart of hearts I knew that the command was for me not to leave my husband. But I took offense and adamantly retorted in my mind, "*I will not stay with a man who has shown no remorse for his actions, I will not!*" Complete silence followed.

Abandoned once again by the sudden stillness, I felt rejected, alone. Rivers of tears fell down my cheeks; the brutal emotional carnival ride of groaning cries and obsessive planning continued until daybreak.

A subtle knock on my door interrupted the neurotic activity; it was Rick. He had heard my mournful cries and wanted to check on me. I was not interested in his compassion and told him to leave.

My mind was racing. I was trying to decide which car I should take, the comfortable Yukon or the smaller economy Mazda for my long trip to Washington. The Yukon would hold more of my things, but what things would I even want to take? While I was mentally packing the car, I was also trying to settle on how I was going to approach the boys to ask whether they wanted to go or stay. What a dreadful dilemma to put my boys in. They were reeling with the shock of this, too. Oh, how I wished this was simply a nightmare and I could just shake myself awake.

I decided. I would take the Yukon. There was another knock at the door, more like a tentative tap. I snapped, "Come in!" My husband was back, and I was ready to give him the full blast of my anger and tell him of my immediate plans. He asked if he could come into the room and sit on the end of the bed. I glared at him and crossly said, "Yes." Putting as much distance between us as possible, I pressed my back against the bedroom wall. Between the convulsive sobbing and screaming tantrums, I began to verbally assault him with all that I had in me. After a few minutes of this brutal expression of my rage, he stood up and walked with reservation to the left side of the bed, just a few feet from me, and asked a very strange question, one that rendered me speechless and silenced my verbal attack.

He asked apprehensively, "Can I hold you?"

The strong but calming voice that had spoken in the night returned to my mind and whispered, "You hold little boys." I am not sure how I can describe that moment. It was like I was in a dreamlike state and could only obey the command, the command I had heard just a few hours earlier. It was as if someone or something took over my mind and mouth in that moment and I stuttered the word, "Yes." But before the word could entirely escape my mouth, Rick collapsed onto the bed, into my arms and wept uncontrollably.

The sorrow that poured out of my husband still moves me today. Even as I write these words my eyes well up with tears. I knew in that moment, in my heart of hearts, that he felt such remorse, such regret for betraying our wedding vows and forsaking our love.

The voice, which I undeniably recognized as God's, knew that I had to be willing to hold the "little boy," the one that was locked deep inside this strong man who had worn a mask to hide his fear and secrets for so many years. Having no understanding at all what this was to mean, I obeyed the command and held my husband as sorrow heaved from this broken man.

Like waves on a violent sea of regret, Rick lamented over and over, "I am so sorry, I am so sorry, I love you so much, I don't want to lose you, I am so sorry." For several days this scenario repeated itself.

God gave me what I asked for. God knew what my heart needed. In order for our marriage to survive and heal from this tragedy, it was crucial that I knew beyond a shadow of a doubt that Rick was heartbroken and repentant for his choices. I also knew that this was only the beginning of the battle that would rage for months, and possibly even for years, as we entered into the wilderness of marital recovery.

My daring decision—and believe me it *was* an act of bravery—to follow the gentle command of my nighttime caller would be just the beginning of my journey. My worst nightmare had come to pass. My life as I knew it was gone, forever altered. So much work had to be done in order for this marriage to survive such a brutal strike. The claws of the terrifying beast had torn through my heart; my hands were stained from the gushing blood.

How would I survive my husband's betrayal?

Decide To Survive

I had a decision to make. Would I continue to collapse under the heaviness of the pain and weight of my sorrows and retreat back into my now dismantled fortress? Would I begin to rebuild the walls that I had so painstakingly demolished or would I decide to take the most frightening and dangerous step of faith and enter into the unknown? Would I choose to face my fears, grab hold of God's hand and allow him to guide me through the unfamiliar wilderness of infidelity?

Many people do not have the courage to begin this journey. Many will step out into the darkness, but because fear overwhelms them, they turn and run for fear of rejection or losing control. Some will venture out, but the moment when the creatures of the dark begin to loom and the voices of their past are louder than the gentle encouragement of their Guide, they disengage and jump off the cliffs of despair for fear of what others might think or what the truth may reveal about them.

You can decide to face the frightening circumstances of your nightmarish life that has threatened to destroy you and your family. You can begin the demolition of false messages and isolating walls that have long held you captive. You can begin letting go of the destructive vices that have caused you to build such strong fortifications that have caused indifference between you and the one you love. You can survive this nightmare that has assaulted your dreams, the dreams of your past and the dreams of your future.

May you have courage, my friend, to survive.

God is out front. He is in our tomorrows,
and it is the tomorrow that fills people with fear.
Yet God is already there.
All the tomorrows of our life have to pass through Him
before they can get to us.

F. B. Meyers

Sometime in your life you will go on a journey.
It will be the longest journey you have ever taken.
It is the journey to find yourself.

Katherine Sharp

The wilderness journey begins.

❤ HEART WORK

Many people experienced a serious lack of security in their childhood family systems. Abuse, infidelity, substance abuse, divorce, or multiple marriages are among things that cause some or all of a child's sense of security to vanish along with their childhood. When events like these happen, we learn to build an emotional fortress, one block at a time. Almost everyone has built a protective wall of some sort around their hearts; some fortresses are higher and sturdier than others. What were the things in your family of origin that may have contributed to the erection of a wall?

Can you see yourself, either now or in your past, hiding behind an emotional protective barrier? If so, picture this wall. As you look at your wall, imagine that each brick represents a protected part of you. For example, one brick might symbolize fear; another might signify an abandonment issue from a childhood event. Other bricks might represent confusion or shame. There are many scenarios that allow our emotional fortresses to be built. When someone or something feels threatening, we get behind our wall for safety. Are you willing to begin dismantling your fortress, one brick at a time? Yes, it is frightening, but the longer you wait, the stronger the fortification will become. The mortar will set and the work will be much more difficult as your heart hardens. Dare to begin breaking down the wall that is protecting your heart right now.

Be careful not to confuse a barrier with a boundary. If you don't know the difference, stop and find the definition of boundary and write it out. Unlike self-constructed barriers, we need good boundaries in place to be healthy.

Write down any thoughts this has triggered in you; be willing to share them with your counselor.

PART II

SURVIVAL GUIDE
CHRONICLES OF A WOUNDED HEART

When your life is threatened, survival is the question.
Once survival is assured, healing is a possibility.

Dr. Craig Bensen[2]

8
FIND TRUE NORTH

The Promised Land always lies on the other side of the wilderness.

Havelock Ellis

Wilderness Nightmare

The moment the words of betrayal fell from Rick's lips, I felt like some unknown force had catapulted my body and mind into a dense, terrifying wilderness of never ending anguish and despair. Harassing, prickly briars would shred my already bleeding and wounded heart even more as this forest of unrelenting sorrow terrorized me. The sinister darkness that now consumed my life would distort my path and cause me to trip and fall as I tried to maneuver around the decayed and twisted limbs that were strewn about the forest floor. I would scream out the "what if" and "why didn't I" scenarios as I lay prostate on the stony path. I would tremble and shake uncontrollably as I stared in unbelief at my ghastly wounds. How is it that I find myself in this wasteland of despair? Could I survive this nightmare?

Many decisions were made along the way, by me and by others that invariably took me down unknown trails of fear, rejection, and abandonment. One trail led to another, the brush became thicker, the air colder, the nights longer— now here I was, aimlessly lost on this path of my husband's betrayal. The endless darkness frightened me. In my mind my life was over. How did I get here, a lost woman of forty-two, married but alone, a mother, a castaway? How did the trails lead to this destruction, this death? Where did I take a wrong turn? How did I find myself so lost and all alone?

I wandered without direction for a time, through the shattered remnants of my life. I would find myself stumbling and crawling through this dark intimidating wilderness, so alone, so frightened, trying desperately to find my way out. But how? How would I find the clearing? Would this trail of sadness and despair ever end? Is there hope for me? Somewhere, somehow, in the midst of this vast emptiness I made a decision. I must survive. My very life depended upon it. If I was going to live through this dreadful wilderness journey that now lay before me, it was vital that I could locate True North. North to me signified my awakening from this nightmarish hell that consumed my life and my mind. To find True North was to find freedom, peace and wholeness, possibly for the first time. If I could find this North, then I knew I could survive.

In my pursuit to find True North, I had to pass through terrifying, wild lands that were occupied by beasts of shame and doubt, and their assaults were constant and vicious.

Their unyielding assaults were set on destroying my life; at times their persistence was more than I could bear. Finding refuge from the mental conflicts would become a daily undertaking. My broken and bleeding heart faced many challenging demands as I continued my search for North. As difficult and painful as my now-altered life had become, with all the uncertainties and fears that now surrounded my shattered world, I unexpectedly stumbled upon many new discoveries, for which I will forever be thankful.

I learned that I did have the strength to grasp a lifeline of hope while violent storms of despair and doom ravaged and tossed my restless mind. I found that I did have the courage; if I chose to move out from among the dark, terrifying cliffs of fear, and I could navigate the deep cavernous caves of confusion that enclosed my wounded soul. As I traversed the brutal mountainside of bitterness and anger, and as the jagged crags of shame tore through my broken heart, I stumbled across the complicated and prolonged route that eventually led to forgiveness. As I traveled along the overgrown pathway toward finding North, I would discover just how strong and resolute I could be. By trial and error I discovered that, without True North as my focus, I would have remained very lost, possibly for a lifetime.

Lost And Found

Have you ever been lost? If not you, then maybe you have experienced a child disappearing in a shopping mall or in one of those chaotic themed pizza parlors where a gigantic mouse roams freely. Unfortunately, I have experienced the harrowing event of losing a child, something I never again want to experience.

It was a hot summer July day; my family had planned as part of our vacation a day at Six Flags amusement park in California. Before we even began our fun filled day of exciting rides and battered corn dogs, Rick and I lost our six-year-old son Luke. I will never forget the fear that came over my whole being as we each thought that the other had our boy. The adrenaline that shot through my system felt as if someone had violently injected me with a warming fluid that caused my chest and face to instantly turn red and burn with intense heat. I felt so much fear, anger and confusion. My mind began devising a scenario that my son had been tricked into taking a carnival toy or cotton candy as a lure by a kidnapper. Horror consumed me at the thought, and I was filled with panic and terror. I remember how my husband and I screamed at each other, *"I thought you were watching him!"* and then, realizing that we were wasting precious time, we put our game plan together to get our son safely back into our arms. I would run with our youngest son Jacob in the stroller to park security and report him missing. My husband, with our oldest son Caleb now glued to his side, would go to the front gates and keep a vigilant eye out for anyone trying to take Luke out of the park.

The waiting—oh, the waiting! It seemed like hours were slowly ticking by. Where was my son?

The report went out that a child was missing, what clothes he was wearing, the color of his hair, and the description of his shoes. Every time I would hear the crackle of the walkie-talkies and hear the voice on the other end, it would make my heart explode with anxiety. I so desperately prayed that I would hear the words, *"We found him!"* I felt as if I was literally going to die; fear and worry consumed me. I wanted to run, but where would I go? I wanted to find my son, but how? What could I do? I felt so helpless, so afraid. I was asked to stay put and wait, so that when Luke was found, I could comfort him.

I tried with all that I had in me to contain my emotions. I could not. Giant tears pooled in my eyes as I slowly rocked Jacob back and forth in his stroller. This rhythmic motion helped divert his busy little body, but in truth it gave me something to do as I silently panicked on the inside.

As I sat on a hard, cold folding chair in the waiting room of the security building, I observed the Lost-and-Found basket in the corner of the room. Miscellaneous items were there. A single white tennis shoe, a well-worn sweater, baby bottles and teddy bears, pacifiers, and watches overflowed the container. These items were insignificant in my mind. A boy was lost—my boy. Those articles of clothing and things were of no value; but a son, the most valuable gift of all, was missing. As I mused over my thoughts it seemed an eternity had passed, but in reality it had only been a few minutes. And then, through the window I saw him. I wondered if my mind was playing tricks on me. I wanted to feel Luke in my arms, to kiss him, to hold him, but it was as if a director of a movie had decided that the reunion would play out in slow motion. The final scene of mother and child arm in arm would have to wait. As the seconds dragged I so desperately wanted to reach out and grasp my young boy; but first, Luke had to be escorted by security personnel through the gray steel door and into my arms. At last, my son had been found.

When our family was intact once again, Rick and I put together the events of this traumatic experience so that we could understand how this could have happened. We remembered that, as we entered the park, we had stopped to look at the colorful cartoon diagram of the huge playground, in order to map out our route for the day. Luke continued on alone, not realizing that we were no longer with him. Mesmerized by the allure of that magical place, he ambled right into the belly of the giant amusement park. Stopping in front of a large water fountain, he watched as other children danced and squealed with delight in the refreshing showers. Suddenly Luke became aware of his situation. He was lost.

Paralyzed with fright, he began to cry. Instinctively Luke knew that he had to find someone who looked as if they could help him, so he promptly located one of the carts with the toys, balloons and delicious pink cotton candy displays that dangled on rods and strings. The observant attendant noticed this frightened little boy and quickly called security. Luke was found.

That moment in time will forever be embedded in my memory. I was determined that never again would I let my boys out of my sight in unfamiliar territory. That emotionally charged event changed the way I mothered forever, but the fear that gripped my son Luke on that hot summer day when he was lost and all alone would haunt him for years to come. Being lost can do that. It can create positive change or build a foundation from which extreme fright will have lasting ramifications, causing a person to become frozen, unable to move forward in certain circumstances.

Shiny Gadgets

I probably should have, but I didn't. If I had paid more attention I would have learned how the device worked. But I was only eleven years old and I didn't realize how important it could be. Now, years later, I realize that it would have been a good idea to know how the tool worked in case I needed to use it someday.

When I was a young Girl Scout I had been instructed on how to use a compass and was told that you should never attempt to go out into the wilderness without a high quality one. Somehow, I did pass the tests to earn my sew-on badges and I proudly wore my accomplishments on my green sash. But I have to be honest; I really did not know how to read a compass. All that seemed to matter at the time was that I could locate True North on my new, shiny gadget.

If you can picture a compass in your mind, it is round, molded from some sort of durable plastic and has a wobbly magnetized needle inside of it. Most needles have a red N printed on the tip or just have a fancy red arrow on one end. The needle swings and rotates because it is balanced on a post, or it is floating on oil or water. Remarkably, the tip points to the magnetic North Pole.

As I reflected back on my life and how I survived my nightmare, it did not take long for me to see the similarities of my insecure self and a wobbly compass needle. As I groped along the unmarked, overgrown trails of despair from my husband's infidelity, I would become uncertain and extremely unsteady in my surroundings. The unstable needle constantly bouncing around pictured my life while I was living out the realities of his choices.

As my life wobbled out of control, I was so desperate, so confused and so weary from trying to fight my way through the unknown territory of betrayal. If I could, (and believe me, at times it took all that I had in me) I would try to allow God to be my compass. I struggled at times to trust in His guidance and I wavered constantly, not understanding why He would lead me to a path that was unclear, covered in thorns. Because of my fears and resulting lack of faith in my Guide, I would find myself repeatedly retracing my steps back through the thick and treacherous undergrowth of my wilderness. Wounds of regret and the abrasions of sorrow were at times my unwelcomed companions as I stumbled and fell on the twisted, cragged terrain.

False Readings

Just as I had learned as a young Girl Scout that it was imperative that I could find True North on my shiny gadget, it was just as critical that I learned to read my compass accurately.

There was one survival tip in regard to my little gadget that I somehow remembered. Because a compass is a magnetic device, you need to stay away from anything iron or steel, like watches, belt buckles and power lines. If you don't, the electromagnetic field will alter the compass. Basically you will get false readings.

Picture a lost hiker trying to use a compass under a power line. The magnetically charged arrow shudders and shakes out of control trying to locate North. Because of earth's powerful magnetic pull and because of the nearby metal object, the needle cannot read properly. As a result the lost hiker stands frozen, not moving for fear that he may go the wrong way.

That is how I lived my life for quite some time. I would find myself near many "magnetic pulls" that hindered me from finding my way through the barren wasteland of my marriage. As I tripped and fell among the brambles and thorns of infidelity, I learned that the powerful and potent emotion of anger, if not dealt with appropriately, would distort and cloud my vision, causing me to become disillusioned with my surroundings. I learned to be very careful with well-intended family or friends' counsel as I trampled and trudged along the dark and despairing trails of confusion. Their advice might not be what was best for me. As I wobbled at times out of control, thoughts of doubt, shame, impatience, and resentment would prey upon my broken heart as I anguished over my husband's choices. Many fraudulent guides deluded me as I tried to navigate my way through the dreadfully unstable terrain; their cunning deceptions caused me not to read my compass accurately. The false reading of fear would become the most terrifying of all as I wandered aimlessly through the wilderness of my broken wedding vows.

These misleading emotions would alter my readings and paralysis would overcome me. Out of fear of not knowing which direction I should go, I would find myself more confused and lost. I had difficulty trying to maneuver around the many false readings that caused my wobbly needle to struggle to find True North.

I felt lost, so very lost. Loneliness consumed me as I groped blindly along my trail of shattered dreams and despairing circumstances. In my struggle to find North, I became suspicious of almost everyone. My heart had been broken, blood flowed from the inflicted wounds and I was wary of letting anyone in too close; I did not want to be hurt again. The process of learning how to trust God, let alone my husband or any other person in my now shattered world, would be one of the most challenging lessons that I had to learn.

I did have a choice however. Would I stay in my paralyzed state? Would I continue to live in the constant chaotic motion of indecision and doubt? Or would I choose to move away from the false readings that distorted my thinking? Just as in my August nightmare, when I mustered up enough strength to shove the cruel, destroying creature of terror away, I was just as resolute to survive this wilderness nightmare. I had to move out from under the magnetic pulls that hindered my ability to read my compass correctly. Somehow I knew that I had to look for North if I wanted to escape from the paralyzing feelings of doom and despair.

This illustration of a compass and the story of my son being lost are portrayals of how, for a season, I lived through my wilderness journey of Rick's betrayal. I would panic often, and then become paralyzed with fear from the trauma of my nightmare. I would scream out in anger and blame God for not protecting me. And then I would try my hardest to stay put and wait in the waiting room of my lost life and strive to let God lead me to North. This unstable reaction of bouncing back and forth from trying to trust to not believing would at times, create great confusion and fatigue. I wondered how I would survive.

Journal Entry, November 22, 2002—2:00 A.M.
> *God I feel scared, please help me!*
> *I don't know what to think, I feel overwhelmed.*
> *Some days, especially the last two weeks,*
> *I can't even remember all that has happened.*
> *What a fog.*

Giving up my beautiful home, my dog, moving into a mobile home way out in the middle of nowhere.

How can we afford gas, electric bills, food?

I haven't felt very close to you lately.

I am scared; I've been spoiled with my life the way it was.

I don't know how to live this new life. Help me! Please!

I need to feel you near me even when I am so far away emotionally ...

God what is wrong with me? I just want to run away and have no responsibilities.

I know that is not possible.

I just need a break God!

HELP ME! HELP ME! HELP ME!

Fill my mind with positive thoughts; I am so afraid ...

Why is this so hard?

I will try to trust you, just "one day at a time."

I will live today, not tomorrow.

Help me live today!

Oh God, help me live today.

Help my mind; help my thoughts; help me to focus on you.

Thank you God, for what I do have.

Help me to remember those things.

Help me to not focus on the past ...

When will the whys go away?

The August 2001 nightmare that terrorized my sleep had become my reality. It was as though my life had literally been destroyed. My heart felt as if it had been torn to shreds by vicious claws and would not stop bleeding. Some days, I wondered if God really existed. In my search for answers to my pain, I wondered if he really cared about my confusion and anger. But one thing was certain: even if I chose not to believe in God's direction, my compass was a good one. It was not a cheap imitation that broke after I threw it down a few times out of sheer frustration of my lost and frightening situation. North was always North; there were no malfunctions with the compass, only in my inability at times to trust where it was guiding me. No matter how distracted I became, or how angry, or how devastated by my sorrow, I could trust my compass, if I chose to do so and pursue True North.

For some unfathomable reason I knew that following God's leading was the only way out of this despairing wilderness of betrayal, so I continued to wobble North. Some days it was not a pretty sight. I would be complaining all along the way, asking questions like, "How much longer?" or "Why, why did this have to happen to me?" And the one grievance that would haunt me relentlessly: "Couldn't you, God, have stopped this tragedy from happening?"

There were days on this journey towards True North that were dreadfully treacherous, with many obstacles and terrors hiding behind cliffs of despair. There were the endless nights with no moonlight to light my path. Those merciless hours of darkness were the most dreadful for me.

I would become enraged with the unrelenting flood of emotions that continually assaulted me. Exasperated by the cruelty of the harassment, I would blame the compass for not leading me in the right direction and then toss the device as if it were of no value to me. What was the result? False readings once again would become my counterfeit guides. Uncertainty, confusion, sorrow and fearfulness would trick my mind and for a time I would listen to their voices of doom, believing when they cunningly whispered, *"This is your life now, learn to deal with it."* After a period of loathing and wallowing in my depressive state, I would once more make the decision to shake the unwanted lies from my subconscious thoughts and trace my path back to where I had flung the instrument. Apprehensively, I would pick up my compass, set my bearings and one more time make a decision to trust in its guidance.

Journal Entry, January 27, 2003
Today I sit looking out my kitchen window.
I cannot see clearly; it is raining.
I am not sure what I am feeling today.
So here I sit, trying to understand my feelings.
I guess I am okay with not understanding.
My life is in your hands God. I will sit where you want me to sit, I will go where you want me to go. Just lead, make it clear.
The windows in this borrowed home have not been clear since the day we moved in.
The condensation slowly drips, just as my heart seeps of sorrow and doubt.
Oh, the lessons I have learned from the fog of winter and unclear windows.

*I must believe, even though everything is
distorted,
I must believe that you God will take care of my
family and me.
I must do my part and trust you with this mess.
I can't see out my windows but I know—just on
the other side of these thin walls of particle-
board and plastic siding—there is a beautiful
landscape out there. There are trees, birds and
mountains. There is life out there!
Okay God, I get it! When nothing makes sense,
when nothing is clear, I must trust you.
I must trust you with my future, my husband, my
kids, and my life!
This will be the ultimate test.
Today, I CHOOSE TO BELIEVE, even if it does
not make any sense, even when it is not clear,
I will choose to believe, today.*

This conversation with God and others like it would
be repeated over and over for quite some time as I struggled with my trust issues. I wrestled with uncertainties, I
panicked often, and I writhed under the strain of my insecurities. I was consumed with doubt and fear every waking and sleeping moment. Minute by minute, day by day,
as I fought my way through the thick and murky wilderness of my lost life, I needed to make a decision. Would
I decide to utilize the faithful compass that had so far
guided me through this nightmare, or would I be paralyzed by the terrorizing creatures of the night and listen
to the false readings of hopelessness and fear.

For me, God is like a good-quality compass. His North will always be constant and correct. He is reliable. He knows the terrain of my wilderness journey. God is a safe and understanding guide, not a cheap substitute for survival. He allowed me to rest when I needed respite. He gently held my trembling hands when I felt I could not reach one more foothold on the steep and slippery mountainside. When I stumbled and fell on the thorny path, God was there. He mended my wounds with gentle and healing balms. God never abandoned me on the despairing trail of shattered dreams and unfulfilled desires. He was my constant companion, even when I felt that he had left me, when I felt completely alone. It was in those moments that I knew that I had to decide to believe, to believe that I would find True North. I chose to believe that I could wait out yet another season of gloomy fog and blind condensation on my heart and mind. God was there; He never left my side.

Journal Entry, August 12, 2003
> *I am learning to trust you God.*
> *Thank you for never letting me down.*
> *Even in those dark, silent days when I wondered where you were, you did not leave me or abandon me.*
> *It was during those deathly, silent days and nights that I grew stronger in my faith.*
> *You are awesome God!*
> *Thank you for always guiding me ...*
> *I have learned that when I pray believing, anything is possible.*

*It might not be the answer that I thought I wanted
or needed at the time, but you answer.*

Thank you! I love you God!

Journal Entry, October 11, 2004

*I have a lot of mixed emotions bouncing around in
my heart, and soul today.*

I feel very disconnected from God.

I feel farther and farther away from his voice.

*I know in my head that God has not gone any-
where, but why the silence?*

Why this feeling of aloneness?

*It feels like I am standing on the edge of a vast
valley—I can see the other side—but how will
I get there?*

*I gaze upon the lush green meadows below. I can
see the various trees that ascend to the rugged,
snowcapped mountains. It is all so beautiful
from this viewpoint, and yet it seems so far
away—unattainable—like I am only supposed
to look upon its beauty.*

So, what does this mean?

*This detachment is very strong; I am not sure
which direction to go.*

*I wish the Lord would open the road map and use
a bright yellow highlighter to mark my path.*

*I know that everything, every event is leading me
somewhere.*

*It would be helpful to have a clear answer, a clear
idea of where I was going.*

What a struggle it has been.

Even in these struggles I am thankful, thankful for
the growth that I've had.
If I had not experienced the many trials and losses
I would not have known God's love and care
for me.
So, here I stand in awe of the beauty of this vast
valley that lies before me.
I know I will make it to the other side one day—
but for today—I will
wait for my Guide to show me the way.

I was lost for a very long time, but eventually I found my way and survived the long journey North! My hope as you continue on this perilous wilderness path towards recovery is that you, too, will find your True North, your *own* awakening from the nightmare that has assaulted your life. My hope for you is that you can learn to put your trust in a Guide that knows your way.

The Lord guides when men are honestly groping.

John Henry Jowett

God, listen to me shout; bend an ear to my prayer.
When I am far from anywhere, down to my last gasp
I call out, "Guide me."

Psalm 61:1-2, *The Message*

I am the Lord your God, who holds your right hand,
and I tell you, "Don't be afraid, I will help you"
... I myself will help you, says the Lord.

Isaiah 41:13-14, *New Century Version*

They will weep and pray as I bring them home.
I will lead them to streams of water.
They will walk on a level road and not stumble.

Jeremiah 31:9, *Contemporary English Version*

❤ Heart Work

In your journal write as much as you can about how lost you feel right now.

What are the character qualities and attributes that would make a trustworthy Guide? Who are the guides in your life that have influenced your journey, both positively and negatively? What are your thoughts about a God that guides? Take a few minutes and write about how you feel about God.

Refer back to the False Reading section of this chapter and think about the people, places, events, or emotions that may have created magnetic pulls in your life. Write about the fear, the shame and the anger that you are feeling right now.

9

HAVE A PLAN

Whatever course you decide upon,
there is always someone to tell you that you are wrong.
There are always difficulties arising
which tempt you to believe that your critics are right.
To map out a course of action and follow it to an end
requires courage.

Ralph Waldo Emerson

Courageous Plan of Action

My husband's confession collided with my already emotionally turbulent life as the vicious claws of betrayal and
deceit tore through my chest. As the heart-wrenching truth
was unveiled, my lifeblood poured out and cruel numbness consumed me. My mind was not capable of reason or
thought. I was certain before this life-altering event that I
knew exactly what I would do. But the plan that I had so

thoughtfully crafted would not be as easily played out as I had practiced in my mind.

When I sequestered myself within the hollow walls of my guest room on the day my worst nightmare terrorized my life, I had intended to divorce my husband. Even though I had clear instruction from the calm invisible voice during the darkest of all nights, early on the question relentlessly harassed my thoughts. *Was I going to stay married to this man who betrayed me or was I going to leave him?* There were many days when I wondered whether I had merely dreamed about the nighttime conversation. Sometimes I wished that I had simply imagined it. I had to make up my mind in order to move forward and survive this nightmare.

The decision I finally made—to stay married and work on our broken issues—would not be the easier choice. As we entered into the strenuous and demanding uphill battle of marital restoration, my counselor told me that this route would be more challenging than if I had left. She was right; I have never fought so hard to stay on course with any decision.

Discerning True Remorse

There is a juncture in this process where the wounded faithful can get stuck or frozen in their pain. When that happens, discernment is vital in order to move forward. This confusing point in time can be brutal to an already fragile mind. You must ask and answer this question: Is my spouse truly repentant for their actions? How do I know for certain? In order for the relationship to move toward healing, this issue must be addressed—not only for the wounded, but for the one who caused the wound as well. I have known many betrayed spouses who made the decision to stay in their traumatized marriages in spite of the lack of that crucial piece of honesty. Typically, the unfaithful one claims to believe his or her affair was not of any consequence. The offending spouse often blames the faithful one. Games continue and their manipulative stories tend to trip up the fragile emotions of the faithful partner. It is imperative that the wounded one is convinced that their spouse's confession, sorrow, and pain are authentic. You will know if it is sincere; trust your heart here. The vow-breakers must fully grasp the impact of the losses that resulted from the infidelity. They must grieve the pain that they have caused your relationship, your lives.

Please remember this: the grieving is not a one-time event. The betrayed and the betrayer will and must mourn, until both reach a sense of renewed peace based on forgiveness. There are many phases in this wilderness walk. You will make many strategic choices to take difficult "steps" before you find complete restoration. This process will take time. You and your spouse will need to learn to be patient with this mourning leg of the journey. During this stage it is common for you to feel lonely, disconnected, and angry.

Impatience will strike. Sometimes you will want this grief process to hurry and be gone. Typically you will wonder why it's taking so long. You will wonder whether it is worth the focused work to stay in your marriage. You will sometimes get very frustrated with your spouse for not working on recovery as diligently and as intensely as you are. Or, maybe you have not put enough time and effort into working on your own issues and your spouse is working harder on personal brokenness. All of this is a part of the journey, the cost of moving forward in a healthy way.

My husband took full responsibility for his infidelity. He made no excuses for his failures or for the pain he caused. That set me up to move forward with my healing. If he had not done this, I would have become stuck in my grief. I knew I could begin to rebuild my life. Otherwise, I would have felt I had fallen into a thick, suffocating pool of quicksand. As I would have tried to escape from the powerful trap of blame and contempt I would only be sucked in deeper, with no hope of getting out. My healing would have been warped and incomplete.

Betrayers must accept full responsibility for the marital disrepair, fixing blame on no one but themselves. They must be willing to seek counsel and discover their brokenness that caused their destructive behavior. They need to join an accountability group or find a same-sex accountability partner to meet with on a regular basis who will help them keep true to the journey towards healing. They must earnestly seek your forgiveness, no matter how long it takes for you to get there. They must be willing to be patient and not put demands on you. They must also learn how to deal with their feelings of anger, as you may need to ask the same questions, over and over.

I remember how I would often forget that I had asked certain questions multiple times, and my husband would answer them repeatedly. Because my brain was so weary from the stress of this trauma, I had not processed his answers, thus making me forget I had asked already. I repeated the crazy cycle over and over. Our offending spouse must be willing to be selfless as we process our pain a spoonful at a time.

Journal Entry, December 10, 2002

> *How much more do I need to bring up and talk about?*
>
> *When will the questions be done?*
>
> *Will I be able to love my husband like I did before?*
>
> *God, help me search my heart and tell Rick my true feelings.*
>
> *Help me not protect him from my emotions, my fears.*
>
> *Help me endure this road that I travel now; please oh, please!*
>
> *I am so afraid that he will do this to me again.*
>
> *How will I ever trust again?*
>
> *What is stopping him from doing it again?*
>
> *Rick just told me that he has what he has always wanted—but I was right beside him—all this time.*
>
> *Help me God!*

If your spouse is in denial or still in the blaming stage, then your journey towards healing will be more complicated and discouraging. You will have to work harder to move forward in your pain. You will need to be in constant communication with a counselor to help guide you towards new life after the marital trauma. Unfortunately, you cannot make a spouse get well or force them to find the motive behind the infidelity, but you can do what *you* need to do in order to heal from this tragedy.

If my husband had not been fully repentant and had not taken total responsibility for the pain that he inflicted, and if he had not been willing to work on his brokenness, my story would have had a different outcome. I knew without any doubt that Rick was truly sorry for his choices. He worked hard on learning how to re-frame the distorted childhood messages that had misled him throughout his adult life. There were times in my recovery that this fact was the one thread of hope that I could hold onto to sustain me while I dangled emotionally from the shock of Rick's unfaithfulness.

As I set out to follow my plan of staying with Rick, there were times when I was too weary to fight and I would buckle under the assaults of emotional mind games that tormented me. Deep feelings of mistrust and low self-worth would assail my thoughts. Prickly brambles of hateful contempt and the razor-sharp thorns of anger occasionally would overcome me. Mental images of my husband's betrayal pierced my mind. Raw emotions would seep through my unsightly wounds. But time and time again I would pick myself up, shake off the dirt of doubt and with resolute fortitude stumble forward.

As I desperately tried to work my plan of moving forward, I would continue to hit this wall of not wanting to feel anything any more. I was mentally and emotionally exhausted. One of the physical signs that clued me in on this numbing behavior was that I would hold my breath for long periods of time, especially at night while lying in bed. My brain would uncontrollably start obsessing with thoughts of the betrayal. I would conjure up in my mind images of what I thought their sinful interludes must have been like. I would be so lost in my made-up stories that I wouldn't even know that I was not breathing until Rick would gently whisper, "Breathe, Patti, breathe!" I later discovered that my breathing problem was an automatic response, signaling to me that my brain was shutting down because I was on emotional overload. When I subconsciously held my breath, for some reason a part of my brain would block the feelings that were trying to scream out at me. I still do not quite understand how that happens. I have noticed that even now, years later, I still tend to hold my breath when I am facing a disturbing thought or difficult circumstance. It is a signal my body provides when I give in to self-pity and feeling betrayed. Evidently my body provides a signal that if I stop breathing my pain will go away.

The darkness of night was the cruelest time of torment for me. My nerves were on high alert. I often would go into rigorous shaking. My immune system was weakened. My body was swollen with maddening hives and yeast infections. Night after night, week after week, as the house was enveloped in darkness and my husband was drifting off to sleep, there was no one to remind me to breathe. It was during those sleepless nights that I struggled more than any other time.

It did not matter how hard I tried, the visions of my husband in bed with another woman haunted my thoughts, and when I could sleep, my dreams. The anguish in my mind was making me feel I was literally going crazy. I worried I would collapse under the strain of the unrelenting torture; my broken mind and heart dripped of despair, misery. There would be no relief. I would beg God to take away the thoughts. I would try to distract myself with anything to tear my bleeding soul away from the repulsive thinking that would consume my brain. I could think of nothing but things like, "Did he say that to her?" When he touched me I would wonder, "Did he touch her there?" "Did she say this or that to him?" "Does he miss her?" "Did she smell good, did she kiss better than I do, did she laugh at his silly jokes?" "How can I ever make love with him again?" "Did he give me sexually trans-mitted diseases?" "Am I attractive? Will I ever laugh again?" I would constantly compare myself to the other woman, thinking that I could never measure up. On and on I would obsess. My pleading with God gave me no respite; my distracting activities did nothing but cause more dread. I was a prisoner of my own mind.

Journal Entry, October 12, 2002
>Oh God! I'm struggling.
>Nighttime is the most difficult for me.
>I can't shut down the thoughts.
>I try so hard, but they keep flooding back.
>I am hurting. I can't believe Rick did this to me.
>How could he?
>I have tried for three days to be strong.
>But God, there is so much more! I have so many questions.
>When will enough be enough?
>How much longer will it be? When will I stop needing answers?
>When can I let it be just be what it is—my husband has been unfaithful?

Journal Entry, November 21, 2002
>When will I believe that it wasn't about sex and wanting other women?
>When will I stop getting visuals about them together?
>When will I feel secure about my own body?
>When do I stop talking to Rick about the past?

When? Please, please,
I beg you to show me, teach me.
Heal me, God.
Please, please, please!

Journal Entry, December 17, 2002
What do I feel today?
I feel a mind struggle.
I am trying hard not to think about what my hus-
band did—trying not to focus on my losses.
Help me to focus on the now, our future.
I wish none of this had happened. I guess I need
to stop saying that, it happened.
Nothing is going to change that.
When will my mind stop going there?
Do I need to keep talking about it over, and over?
I am not sure how I am supposed to react to my
tormenting thoughts.
Do I push them away, or do I allow my brain to
think them?
How do I deal with this God?
I wish you would just tell me.
How can a person forget such pain?
I know it will not hurt as badly one day, but how
do I forget?
When I try to look forward my mind goes numb.
Please God; don't let him hurt me like this again.

Confront the Obsessing Evil

After many attempts to try to move forward in my
tainted life, and after numerous screaming episodes at God

to take away the excruciating anguish, I stumbled onto a method that seemed to work for me. Instead of doing everything in my power to make the thoughts go away, which did not work, I came to the conclusion that the only way for me to get past the crazy and obsessive thinking was to will myself to face each thought, each memory and every sting of betrayal that would assault my mind, stare at it right in the face and not flee from the pain.

"Face it.

Embrace it.

Mourn it,

Move on." (Repeat as often as needed.)

This almost poetic self-talk was easy for me to remember and it worked. I will be honest. This strategy took time, and great effort. At times I wasn't sure that I could stick with this plan of facing each pain head-on. I believe that the mental self-discipline that I poured into this act-of-the-will was one of the most important parts of my recovery. I would have to force myself to continue moving forward and to be willing to face the excruciating pain. My brain would become exhausted, my body weary, but I was determined to move forward. So I would repeat the self-talk affirmation over and over for many months, until eventually this repetitive practice worked for me.

Journal Entry, February 1, 2003
This morning I started thinking again.
Not like before, not about the details,
but about the timing of when all of this took place.
I feel so much pain.
The pain I feel for our boys and their losses is
excruciating.

I grieve the losses and I move on.
Sometimes I get so tired of the mental work
I have to do.
But I am determined to get down the road with
this new life that is now before me.

Approaching Upheaval

There were days when I did not feel I belonged anywhere on this planet. I felt alone, completely cut off from the world. During that difficult season there was only one place where I felt alive. That place was on our twenty-four acre farm. We had aspirations of building our dream home there, but all planning had been put on hold. We were not sure how long we were going to be able to keep our land.

One day I drove to our farm and sat in my Yukon gazing out across our farmland. The cold February winds began to blow and I watched as approaching storm clouds swirled and churned on the horizon. As I openly poured out my thoughts and feelings to God, I sat with pen in hand and documented each one in my tattered notebook.

Feeling chilled, I turned the ignition. The vibration of the engine and the gentle hum of the heater calmed me. I waited for some sense of direction. I desperately pleaded with God to guide me.

Journal Entry, February 3, 2003
I read somewhere that the pain will leave as
I learn to see you God in all things.
How can the pain leave? It feels so raw.
I guess I want the pain to leave right now!

I am human; I know that would be impossible.
So God, I do know that you are in all of this.
I also know that I did not deserve this pain.
Now, help me to grow from this.
What am I supposed to do now?
Where do I go from here?
Do I need to go away for a while—distance myself
from my husband? Let my heart heal?
What do I need to do?
I know in this moment that I am doing the right
     thing—sitting, waiting.
But God, I need you to show me the way.
Tell me what I am supposed to do now.
Comfort me, please! I need you.
Where are you God?
I will wait, and listen.

And then it happened. As the storm clouds released their pent-up pressure and raindrops started to fall on the windshield, distorting my vision, something shifted. My thoughts were becoming clearer, more concise; it was as if God was gently lifting a veil that had been covering my heart, my mind. I could see.

Okay, I get it. I need to stop hanging on to all my
     losses.
I try letting them go, then I seize them again,
     gripping them tightly.
Why do I hang on?
How can I truly let them go?
I am hurting myself; I will not heal if I choose to
     cling to my losses.

I must mourn them; grieve them once and for all.
I must not fight any longer.
The tighter I hold on, the more I get tangled in this
*   ugly web Satan spun to harm me.*
I will win this; I will not be defeated!
I accept this pain God. I accept it!
I will never ask you to remove it from me again.
I will accept and not fight. I will let go.
I do not want to hold on to my losses anymore.
The pain is too intense.
I accept this journey God. I will not ask you "why?"
I will not look back and wish it could be different.
Now I can move on. This is behind me—a new
*   chapter, a new life!*

The following day another storm was brewing, a different kind of fury was approaching. Little did I know that the great victory I had felt just the day before would be tested so soon, so violently.

I had just left my counseling session; it had been a difficult one for me. Reality had hit and my heart had been shattered once again. This time the damage seemed to be beyond repair.

Journal Entry, February 4, 2003
*   I just finished with counseling, I feel so sad—so*
*   numb.*
*   I got in my car and started driving.*
*   It is so strange to drive and have no place to go.*
*   I didn't want to go home—the mobile home is not*
*   my home.*

Because of my emotional state I really shouldn't be behind the wheel of a car.

I am not thinking clearly right now.

The only place that I have that is my own is the farm.

So here I sit once again, just like yesterday, staring off into the stormy horizon.

I've cried so much these last few days—I catch myself not breathing.

Why am I so troubled, so sad?

Yesterday, I was willing to let go of my loses, but there is still so much pain.

Today my counselor said that when Rick confessed my marriage died.

I feel like I died with it.

Who was I?

Who am I now?

I have no idea.

My marriage is dead, now I have to restart and I don't know how.

All I have are memories and bad habits.

I feel like I have skipped a whole stage of my life, never to get it back; no do over's.

I know that Rick is a better man now; I know that he loves me but something is missing, and I don't know what it is.

Is this what death feels like—this vast emptiness?

I don't feel that I can be the wife that my husband really wants.

> *I wasn't what he wanted before so how can I*
> *please him now—now that I am so lost and I*
> *can't even find me.*
> *God, I feel such despair.*
> *Help me so I can go on, what is my next step?*
> *How can I rebuild?*
> *No, how can I begin a new marriage with Rick?*
> *I don't know what to do, where to start.*
> *I feel like I am sinking into a black hole.*
> *It is not depression. I have been there.*
> *This is so different.*
> *I feel like my whole life is being squeezed out of*
> *me.*
> *My heart feels all twisted and mangled, like*
> *someone has a death grip and will not*
> *let go.*
> *I hold my breath so I cannot feel the pain.*
> *This is not a feeling of wanting to die; it is like*
> *I have already died.*
> *How long God? How long?*
> *I need hope God. I need hope.*

Little by little I felt I was tumbling backward as I struggled against the powerful assaults of the unrelenting storms in my new life. I felt I was being plunged right into the belly of a violent hurricane. How would I make it through this pounding, unyielding force?

But without fail, as soon as I believed that I could not go on, God would reveal himself to me just in time. The prevailing winds would die down, my confusion would begin to wane and once again I would pursue True North. But this time, the bright red N was found through the comforting words of an author.

In the midst of my anguish, on the day I realized that my marriage had died, I read the following excerpt from my faithful companion, the book, *"Streams in the Desert"* by L. B. Cowman:

> The sufferings of life are God's winds. Sometimes they blow against us and are very strong. They are His hurricanes, taking our lives to higher levels, toward His heavens.
>
> Do you remember a summer day, when the heat and humidity were so oppressive, you could hardly breathe? But the dark cloud appeared on the horizon, growing larger and larger, until it suddenly brought a rich blessing to your world? The storm raged, lightening flashed, and thunder rumbled. The storm covered your sky, the atmosphere was cleansed, new life was in the air, and your world was changed.
>
> Human life works exactly on the same principle. When the storms of life appear, the atmosphere is changed, purified, filled with new life and part of heaven is brought down to earth.[3]

I did survive yet another storm, but this time the lessons I learned forever changed the way I would handle the next emotional upheaval. I knew there would be more strong winds that would rage; another tempest would blow through the canyons of my life. But fortunately I now had a plan; my motivating self-reminder, "Face it. Embrace it. Mourn it. Move on!" worked every time as I faced each sudden and pounding assault.

As difficult as these lessons were, I finally understood. Storms of life are productive. They clean the air of the impurities that hinder our progress. The invigorating, refreshing scent of the earth after the showers have washed away the dust and debris is stimulating. New life is revealed, a brighter, more vibrant life is available if I choose.

Journal Entry, February 5, 2003
> *Well God, I have been to hell and back over the last few days.*
> *I see your hand again!*
> *The fury of this storm has ravaged my mind, my heart and my life.*
> *Thank you for watching over my storm.*
> *I know that you allowed me to go through this despair to bring me to a higher place.*
> *I had to come to the place where I could truly let go of all of my losses.*
> *Now I understand that it does not mean that I will forget them.*
> *I always struggled with that part.*
> *I discovered that "letting go" means to take my white-knuckle grasp off.*
> *Not holding onto my losses prepared the way for the floodgates of mourning to open.*
> *I have to mourn.*

I can't mourn something that I am not willing to give up.

Now I am mourning the losses. They are forever gone.

No do-over's, no regrets.

No more "if I had only____." no more "if Rick had only____."

No more blaming.

Just gone.

My counselor was right; my marriage died the day that my husband confessed, and I died with it.

And now I must mourn those losses.

So, once again I will sit and let you guide me God.

I will not move from this place in my heart and soul until you show me what the next step is.

I will try to trust you God.

I will not run from the pain.

Help me to ride the winds of this storm.

Face It. Embrace It. Mourn It. Move On.

This was the plan that I chose, and this is how I learned to face my losses and move forward in my wilderness journey. I would embrace my pain; I would mourn the loss until it did not have its death grip on me. Then I would choose to let go and move on. I chose to release in order to move forward. In the beginning I had to will myself to practice this method. After some time the process went from an hourly ritual to a daily routine to a once-in-awhile refresher course of mourning to move forward. I knew that I just had to do this; I was tenacious, and I wanted to get on with my life.

I could have reneged on my plan of action, I could have listened to the dark voices at night that would scream at me with threats of hopelessness and despair; but instead, even though it went against all of my intellect, I tried to listen to the one voice, even though at times it may not have been very clear. Somehow I knew that God would understand my fears and awkward ramblings of disbelief and anger, and if I would not give up, I would get through this season of pain.

Thoughts for the Wounded Heart

This time in my healing would prove to be one of the most challenging phases thus far. This leg of your journey may be just as difficult for you to navigate as it was for me. Do you have a plan? Do you have the courage to stick with the plans that you have chosen? Some days you, too, may feel you are not making any progress; at other times you may have no sense of direction and you feel completely lost, or you may have fallen off of your path entirely. Work diligently at finding your trail again. Put your plan into action once more. Pick yourself back up and dust the doubts away.

If you can work through the barriers that have blocked your path, if you can choose to trust in the quiet voice that speaks in the darkest of nights, you will be able to navigate the long, perilous road toward a healthy life, toward the relationship that you have so long desired.

Sometimes, in your foggy mental state, you may feel your plan of action does not make any sense. In reality, at times nothing seems to make sense at many points along this journey. But if you choose every minute, every hour, to push past the pain, just one more time, you will eventually move on to the next step of survival. This will take time. It will take more courage than you think you have and then, one day the fog will lift, the storm clouds will dissolve, and your path will become clearer.

There are some things that you learn best in calm,
and some in storm.

Willa Cather

But God saves those who suffer through their suffering.
He gets them to listen through their pain.
God is gently calling you from the jaws of trouble
to an open place of freedom ...

Job 36:15-16, New Century Version

Storms have hurt you ... but I will rebuild.

Isaiah 54:11, New Century Version

♥ HEART WORK

The word repent in the ancient Greek means to make a 180° turn and begin to move in the opposite direction. Has your spouse turned 180° from the direction he or she was going, expressing true repentance and sorrow for all the pain inflicted upon you? How do you know for certain? If you have stayed with your spouse, what are some road signs that indicate that a turn in direction has taken place? Continue to document your thoughts regarding this vital issue and what it might mean about the current status of your relationship?

Get away by yourself and in quiet solitude listen with your heart. Write your thoughts down regarding what you believe your plan will be. Do not allow anything to distract you from this important quiet time. Whether you have stayed with your spouse or not, it is important to have a plan of action. Decide what your plan needs to be. Be thorough and firm with your decision. Where do you want to be, say, a year from now on this journey? How do you think you can best get there?

You may want to take your journal to your next counseling session for further discussion.

10

ENDURANCE

Surviving meant being born over and over.

Erica Jong

Pain Without Scars?

I woke up to the high pitched sound of my four-year-old son Caleb screaming, "Mommy's dead! Mommy's dead!" I am not sure how I got from inside the car to lying on the uneven, rocky ground. Rick was hovering over me; I could faintly see the blue sky above the canopy of trees, my surroundings seemed foggy, voices muffled. I heard sirens in the distance.

Many years ago I was a passenger in a car, the driver was going too fast for the upcoming curve and we slid off the gravel road, over the embankment and hit a large fir tree head-on. The impact catapulted my body towards the dashboard and my forehead shattered the windshield, causing terrible facial wounds and a severe concussion. As a result I was hospitalized for a couple of days.

During my hospital stay I had two nurses caring for me, each with a unique personality. My daytime caretaker seemed quite angry. It felt to me that she did not like her job very well and was just making her rounds to get through her day. When this troubled woman would come into my room to do her routine checks, one of her duties was to clean my abrasions. She would roughly scrape the forming scabs and infection from my facial wounds with medicated gauze as if she was scouring a pot. I remember wishing I had the courage to say out loud, "Could you scrub a bit softer please?" But instead, I held firmly onto the handrails of my hospital bed, withheld my comments and moaned with pain.

Now the night shift nurse, on the other hand, was definitely in the right profession. He would enter my room like an angel floating on a cloud. Well, maybe that was the pain medication playing tricks on me, but I do remember how he genuinely nurtured and cared for me. My nighttime cherub meticulously and tenderly scraped my abrasions, and then with great gentleness he applied healing antibiotic ointment. Because of his soothing care I felt virtually no pain. I lay there in my bed, actually enjoying the process.

After I was released from the hospital, and as the swelling and bruises faded away, I was amazed and totally grateful to see that there were no scars on my face. I believe that even though the two nurses had different techniques, one quite painful and the other somewhat soothing, the two methods they used were quite productive. With their harsh scrubbing and gentle rubbing, they were able to work out the infection and massage the damaged skin without leaving me with disfiguring facial scars.

Those same two nurses were in my recovery room after each one of my boys was born, I am sure of it! If you have given birth to children you know what I am talking about. One nurse briskly and painfully kneads your flabby belly while telling you all the while that they must manipulate your uterus after childbirth, and the other nurse gently but just as effectively massages the blood, tissue and muscles in your uterus but without using so much force. Both methods do the job—one we complain about, the other we grin and bear as we wait out the uncomfortable moments so we can get on with our life at home with our newborn baby.

As I continued on this journey towards a healthy life after betrayal, I had to learn to endure the different types of healing processes while I recovered, in order to heal from the wounds with the least amount of scarring. Some of these methods were gentle and soothing; at other times the process was quite harsh and abrasive. If I would allow the healer who knows me to heal my wounded soul, and if I could bear the pain a little longer, then I knew I would be able to get on with my life, the life that I so desperately wanted to live.

Embrace the Pain

One of the most excruciating and abrasive parts of recovery for me was practicing the plan of action I had chosen: face it, embrace it, mourn it, and move on. At times facing my pains head on and allowing the mental images to be right in front of me was some of my most difficult work. It would take all the courage and willpower I could find to go to that place in my mind, to force my brain to visualize my husband's cruel betrayal.

After trying either to numb myself or to distract my thoughts, which never worked, I learned to stare down the pain. I would face it. Then I would say out loud, sometimes even scream," Okay, bring it on!" This would happen numerous times a day, even during inopportune times, such as driving. I learned to seize the pain, hold on to the loss, visualize the offense, and feel the repulsion, anger, and disgust of the actions!

I know this method sounds crazy, but this practice worked for me. I had to feel the pain and agony of the tragedy that had invaded my world and tormented my mind. I had to become skilled at not minimizing it; if I did, it would only prolong my grief. I learned to embrace the pain!

Journal Entry, October 31, 2002
  I have struggled all yesterday, and today.
  I realized in the last couple of hours that the shock
    of all of this is starting to wane.
  The reality has set in and I AM ANGRY!
  I AM ANGRY!
  How could Rick have done this to me, to the boys,
    to our life?
  Why?
  I don't even know who my husband is.
  I can't stand the pain. Sometimes I wish I could die.
  Who were you? You led a double life.
  How could you do that?
  How could you pretend that you loved me?
  How could you?
  I know that your childhood has a lot to do with it
    and I will have to learn to deal with that, but

it is hard to separate the man who could have
said "No."
God tried to help you, but you would not listen.
Why? Will I ever understand?
I am so angry that you destroyed my world
and I have to be punished over and over again.
I have to do all of the work of packing up the
house to move, I have to clean, and I have to
decide what to do with our pets.
The shock has worn off.
Now I feel the raw emotion of what has happened.
My heart is broken.
How could you have been so stupid, so selfish?
And all the while you made me look bad;
like it was my entire fault.
What abuse—to my mind—to my heart!

Journal Entry, February 2, 2003
I have been robbed of EVERYTHING!
I feel like I will never have the joy I could have had.
Will this ever, ever go away? I am hurting so badly.
I am so tired of this rollercoaster ride, I WANT TO
GET OFF!
I now know why Rick would not hold me at night,
why he didn't want to be with me. He didn't
want me.
He didn't want me. Oh God, I feel so much pain,
so much loss.
I know; I know I need to forget about the past,
think about my future.

How can I think about our future when everything we do as a couple I know he did with her? How can I continue to live this life?

It seems like I am always messing up our dates.

Do we not go out anymore?

I do not know what to do; I want desperately to have a new life.

How can I do that, when all I can think about is what he did with her?

I need help!

I want off this ride!

I am sitting here thinking and thinking—and I realize—I need to put the blame where blame belongs.

I have been saying all along that she robbed me.

NO! My husband robbed me!

Now, what do I do with that thought?

Rick robbed me. What do I think about that?

It makes me angry, sad, and depressed.

I am afraid.

Mourning to Move Forward

Once I faced the offenses and embraced my pain, I would then mourn my many losses. I had to feel the emptiness that had taken me captive. I cried, I wept, until I had no more tears. I allowed the mourning to flood my soul.

I would encourage you, as well, not to hinder this process. You must mourn in order to heal. Holding on or holding back to protect yourself only prolongs the recovery of your tragedy. Mourn out loud. Scream out at the losses; let them hear you!

I once sat in a motel parking lot and did not leave until I had mourned the loss of my husband meeting her there for an afternoon rendezvous. I did not care how crazy I must have looked, sitting in the car screaming at the two of them. After what seemed an eternity, I was emotionally drained, but the power of that place no longer had its grip on me. I faced my pain, mourned it totally and was ready to move on.

> *Journal Entry, November 6, 2002, 4:30 AM—can't sleep*
> *God! I feel like I am going to explode.*
> *My head hurts from all of the crap in it!*
> *I keep thinking why did all of this have to happen?*
> *Then I think how could my husband be with another woman?*
> *I have to give up everything—my home, my dog, and my life.*
> *Oh, how my heart hurts!*
> *My life is in such turmoil. I don't like being a mother right now.*
> *I just want to go and hide somewhere. HELP ME GOD!*
> *Help me please.*
> *I need something—something—I don't even know what.*
> *I need something that holds a light in this darkness—something that will help me cope.*
> *When will my heart stop hurting?*
> *Please help me.*
> *I can't do this.*

Journal Entry, November 2002

Lord, I don't even know what today is, November 10th or 11th?

I am not sure.

We've been moving to the mobile home. It will be a nice home I guess.

I am still struggling over losing so much; moving is so stressful.

I can't sleep again. It is now 1 AM. My brain will not shut off.

I think about them together. Why, why can't I let this go?

Please Lord I need your help. It hurts so badly.

I feel deep sadness. I know that it is over, but why can't I let it go?

Help!

My husband said to me that he would never hurt me like this again.

Can he really say that? Really? How does he know?

Oh, God—so many losses. When will the pain go away?

How long will this take? Will I always hurt?

I need to let go of the past. I have a future, right?

You are going to let me have a future, right?

I feel so insecure about everything, my life, my future, my boys, my husband, my job, and my home.

My world is turned upside down—shaken.

Does my husband really love me?

Really?

What do I know?

Mourning, I move forward. I persevere, even when the raw and opened wounds of my heart ooze like painful blisters and my mind feels bruised and broken beyond repair. I keep pressing on to my goal: hope for a future where I will be loved and I can love in return.

When an athlete is training for a marathon or a mountain climber is preparing for the big climb, it is imperative that they can withstand long periods of prolonged exertion or pain. They must keep pressing forward to reach their goal. It is the same with infidelity. I learned that in order for me to survive, despite the ravages of time, I needed to mourn until I was finished. I knew when I was done. I learned not to stop the flow of emotion, fears, or anger. I trained myself not to be afraid of this process. This would prove to be yet another difficult part of my healing. It seemed there would be many challenges as I journeyed ahead into the unknown.

Monumental Marker

Another method that seemed to help me move forward with my struggles of facing my pain and embracing my losses was to build an altar. You might call it a memorial marker made of stones. I collected the stones in an uncultivated area on our farmland, beneath an old weather-beaten tree. This approach may sound silly or even outlandish. I had read about this kind of a memorial marker, and I was desperate to try anything to help me move forward with my pain. So I followed the advice, and I built a memorial marker.

This exercise of laying stones one on top of another gave me something to hold onto as I mourned the loss of what I thought I had. I would grieve over my past, my future, my memories and my dreams. I gave each pain a name.

The first stone was for my boys. I groaned deeply for my children's emotional wounds and their many losses. I then laid a stone for my shattered dreams of the past and another for my future—a future now blemished with betrayal. I placed a stone for the broken promises in the wedding vows that we had exchanged and another for anniversaries, holidays and vacations that now seemed so tainted and stained. One rock at a time I built a memorial in that field on a cold winter day.

I stood up from the frozen ground and blinked through dripping tears as I stared down upon my pile of memories. The emotion and tears that poured out of me on that cloudy day were healing. This stony pile signified the day I chose to move beyond this life that seemed to be smothered in pain. I had a visual symbol of my willingness to walk down this path to recovery.

I wish I could have somehow gathered up that memorial just to keep the image in front of me after we sold the land. The memory of that day is a fond one. It is lodged deep within the crevices of my heart and mind. Now, years later, I have often wondered if the marker might still be there in that field of alfalfa and if the new owners who bought our land may have been puzzled about the meaning of a pile of rocks under the old elm tree. Maybe they thought it was a gravesite for a treasured pet. Little would they know that, yes indeed, it was a burial place, but for the tragic loss of shattered dreams and broken promises. They wouldn't have guessed that it was not just a marker for death but also a symbol of new life as well.

Whether you decide to build a rock memorial out in the middle of nowhere or you scream at your losses, I encourage you to find whatever will work for you. However you decide to move forward in your pain, remember mourning will take time. Do not rush it. You may need to mourn the losses again and again, depending on the extent of your injury. Eventually the death grip of pain will begin to diminish and loosen its hold on you.

> *Journal Entry, December 2, 2002*
>> *Sometimes, I feel like my whole life has gone before me.*
>> *Sometimes, I feel joy and other times there is so much pain.*
>> *I wish that my husband had not betrayed me.*
>> *I wish I could have had 22 years of incredible memories.*
>> *I wish I did not have to experience so much loss.*
>> *God, help me to dwell on the good, on the gifts you have given.*
>> *Thank you for all that you have done for me ...*

Moving On

Somehow I had to move forward, but accomplishing this was very difficult for me at first. I had to start my life all over, but how?

I am a picture freak. I have thousands of photos saved on my computer's hard drive, I have multiple albums on shelves, and scattered throughout my home I have various photos on display. In each home that I have lived in, I created a wall for my immediate family; and if the home had built-in shelving, I would exhibit old photographs from both sides of our families in antique frames. These pictures were important to me;

they represented a happy time, a good memory. That is why these treasured memory keepers deserve beautiful frames, capturing those moments for all time.

Because my life prior to my husband's confession was such a confusing mess, I often felt overwhelmed and emotionally drained. During that season of life, while I was dusting and cleaning I would often pause to stare into a photo and reflect on its memory. Like a mini-vacation in my mind, each photo reminded me of a happier time. It is amazing how much power a photo can have. It can launch you right back to the place and time when it was taken. You can almost hear the sounds or feel the feelings that were evoked in each one. I found that this was just one way I would escape from my world of pain. Even if pain was on my mind, I found peace in those mini-vacations.

When my world exploded, I found some of those photos induced a new kind of memory. The sudden rush of anger would exacerbate my sorrows even more. Looking into my husband's face, frozen within the wooden and metal frames, I could only see a poser, a fraud, staring back. This would be too difficult for me. So for a time, I painfully removed some of the pictures and stored them in boxes, completely out of sight. This was especially difficult for me, as some of the photos included our boys.

Oh, how I would mourn, not only for myself, but for my sons as well. Their lives were also mangled and torn by this nightmare; but in order for me to process my pain and move on, I had to make some very unpleasant decisions. It would be a couple more years of wilderness journeying before I could haul the boxes back out and display the photos once again.

Re-Create

During that time of embracing my pain and mourning to move forward, I was almost obsessed with trying to make new memories. I frantically tried to create photo opportunities to replace the pictures that were now in boxes and placed in closets. I felt that these new pictures in new frames would help fade out the memory of the old. This worked for me.

Creating new memories is an important way of enduring through the raging and tormenting pain of the present and past. If you have stayed with your spouse and if it is feasible, revisit the place where you first met. Return to the exact spot where you kissed for the first time, rekindle that moment in your history together. Perhaps there is a special park or restaurant from your past that holds fond memories. If finances permit, take a vacation and start a new collection of sentimental souvenirs and photos. Purchase a digital frame to display your new adventures.

If your spouse has chosen not to do the work and move forward towards a healthy relationship and you are alone on this journey, you can begin to create new memories for yourself.

Buy season tickets to the theater or sporting events, join a cooking class or learn to dance. Take up a hobby that you have been afraid of doing, like painting or pottery. Dare to trigger-start something new. Find the courage to take a chance again.

I believe that as you try to survive this nightmare and as you struggle to move forward in your pain, making new memories for yourself will be like a healing balm that soothes your wounded heart. Yes, it will be difficult at first to step out and discover your new life, but the outcomes are worth it. You will cherish your new memories; I can vouch for that. My home now has on display photos that memorialize both past and recent memories; they have woven together nicely in the fabric of my new life.

Endure

Have you embraced your pain? Stared it straight in its face? Have you named each painful experience and mourned the tremendous loss it has caused? Can you boldly scream at your losses? Do you dare create new memories for yourself that will nurture your wounds so your heart and mind can begin the healing process?

Let me encourage you to be afraid and to feel the pain and to be willing to acknowledge the hurt and anger as a part of your healing. But most importantly, please remember this: you must not try to rush this process. Take the time this part of your journey deserves.

Endure, my friend. You can do this. Your pain and suffering will not be wasted.

I'll never forget the trouble,
the utter lostness, the taste of ashes,
the poison I've swallowed.
I remember it all—oh, how well I remember—the feeling of
hitting the bottom.
But there's one other thing I remember, and remembering,
I keep a grip on hope:
God's loyal love couldn't have run out,
his merciful love couldn't have dried up.
They're created new every morning. How great your
faithfulness!

I'm sticking with God (I say it over and over).
He's all I've got left.
God proves to be good to the man, who passionately waits,
to the woman who diligently seeks.
It's a good thing to quietly hope, quietly hope for help
from God ...
When life is heavy and hard to take, go off by yourself.
Enter the silence. Bow in prayer.
Don't ask questions: Wait for hope to appear.
Don't run from trouble. Take it full-face.

Lamentations 3:19-29, *The Message*

God keeps an eye on his friends,
his ears pick up every moan and groan.
Is anyone crying for help?
God is listening, ready to rescue you.
If your heart is broken, you'll find God right there.
If you're kicked in the gut, he'll help you catch your breath.

Psalm 34:15,17-18, *The Message*

No one ever told me that grief felt so like fear.

C.S. Lewis

❤ HEART WORK

Are you willing to face, embrace, and mourn your heart pains? What can you do today that will help you mourn your losses? (I went to a motel parking lot.) Do you dare to face the betrayal head on and scream at your losses?

Try this exercise. As you face (think about) the event and/or the person who has created the heart pain in your life, write the feeling words down. Embrace those feelings. Say out loud, "I feel_____." (Use the feeling list if you need to.) FEEL the pain that each thought or feeling word evokes. You may need to repeat this several times in order for you to mourn adequately, but it will eventually open you up to move on. If you get stuck with one or more of the emotion words, be sure to take that information to your counselor.

What new memories can you create for yourself in order for the process of "moving on" to begin? If you have stayed in the marriage and indifference was a large part of your relationship, try doing things completely differently than you did before this marital trauma. For instance, one week you would plan an outing or date, and the next week your spouse would do the planning. If weekly dates are not feasible, then alternate who plans the date on a monthly basis.

Create a bucket list—meaning, you write down as many things that you would like to do as a couple or individually and throw them in a bucket, so-to-speak. Dream big here; then plan to do at least one every few months or so. Make sure to capture the memories along the way by taking photographs to document your new life from this point forward.

11

Discern the Situation—Trust Your Instincts

It is only with the heart that one can see rightly, what is essential is invisible to the eye.

Antoine de Saint-Exupery

Choices

In order to trust my instincts after my husband's confession, I had to make some difficult decisions. This was not an easy thing for me to do. What if I did not make the right choice? What if my husband refused to work on his broken issues? Am I a fool for believing that my marriage can survive?

I have shared throughout this guidebook that, as I navigated my way through the many paths this wilderness walk laid out before me, I would find it difficult to decipher what my heart and head were trying to tell me. At times the trail was hard to follow. How would I know which way to go? Journaling my confusing thoughts and feelings in my notebook was the only way that I could unlock the madness that consumed me.

For me, the process of writing is similar to my visits to ocean or lake beaches. Every time I have an opportunity to visit a beach, I find myself meandering down the shoreline trying to find the perfect piece of driftwood or a large fallen log. Once my waterfront seat is located, I will then squirm and shift my bottom to fit into the various nooks and crannies of the wood to find a comfortable position. Once I am settled I begin staring out to the horizon, becoming hypnotized by the rhythmic motion and sound of the waves crashing onto the shore. Then without realizing it, I will scoop up a handful of warm sand and let it slowly trickle and flow between my fingers. The ritual is always calming and soothing, I would lose myself in my thoughts.

Journaling is like that for me—comforting, consoling, and reflective. However, there were times when writing down my thoughts was not enough. It was helpful to get my feelings out of my mind and out where I could see them, and yet there were times when my emotions and crazy thoughts would continue to bounce around, creating an environment for doubt and indecision. I thought I would go mad. I needed help. During this period of conflicting emotions I discovered an added element to journaling that enabled me to better discern what my heart was trying to say to me. The directions were simple. After writing in your journal read it back to yourself, out loud. Not knowing all of the psychology behind this practice, I learned that there is a part of our brain that does not hear our thoughts except when our words are spoken out loud. That practice helps our subconscious mind awaken and begin to process what we are feeling. So I gave it a try and I began to read out loud to myself what I had written, and it seemed to work.

When I would take the time for myself and write my feelings and frustrations down on paper, it was like entering into a safe haven from my chaotic world. But, it was when I began to read my written words out loud, that the flood of emotion would overflow and, amazingly, I could get a sense of what my heart was feeling. I found this method to be very helpful and beneficial to my heart *and* my mind, which in turn helped me learn to trust my intuitions.

Survival Instincts

Imagine for a moment that you have had no survival training and you found yourself lost in some vast mountainous region. Even with no prior instruction your survival instincts kick in. Perhaps you have watched a television show or you have heard survival stories of people lost in the woods, and it gives you just enough nerve to believe that you can get through the first night on your own. If by chance you do not have a trusty compass, and you cannot find your bearings, you would probably scout out the landscape and find a hollowed-out stump from a fallen fir tree. You would arrange plenty of pine boughs and moss for bedding, knowing that this would provide shelter and warmth so you could endure the cold, bitter night. You would almost certainly gather berries, pine nuts and mushrooms to give yourself proper nourishment during the daylight hours.

You are now set. Yes, you are frightened beyond belief and exhausted from the emotional and physical weight of your situation. As hard as it may be, the experts say you must stay put and wait out your rescue, unless of course you do not have available water. Then it is advised that you must go out and find this valuable life-sustaining resource, possibly having to leave your camp and move on to a better, safer location.

Astonishingly, over the years I have read in the headlines, and I have witnessed, dramatic rescue events unfold on the news—Search and Rescue teams coming across a lost person wandering aimlessly on an abandoned logging road. If they had not thought through the ramifications of their situation, whether they should stay put or move forward, the outcome may not have been so celebratory.

Exposure

Any time that we are in the wild, we should be on the alert, attentive to our surroundings. We have been born with strong natural instincts, and we are wise when we heed our intuitive gut feelings. There could be danger lurking, and these intuitions help us discern whether or not we are safe.

If you have ever been in the wilderness taking a hike, or even camping overnight somewhere deep in the woods, then you know of the quandary of not having the convenience of outhouses and anti-bacterial gel. I have, and I can recall the anxious feeling of being an easy target as I wandered through unfamiliar woods looking for the ideal placement of logs and shrubs that would give me the proper screen to relieve myself. I would eventually find that perfect spot, and then cautiously I would look and listen for anything or anyone that might jump out from behind the evergreen trees and large boulders to try to harm me while I was in this very exposed position.

When I think of the meaning of exposure, it makes me think of being unprotected, vulnerable, that there is some risk involved, that something harmful could happen if I linger too long. We have learned from a very early age that we must protect ourselves from anything that may harm us, like too much sun exposure, or toxic chemicals, or approaching storms. Being exposed may not be healthy; it can be painful, even quite detrimental. We've been instructed to wear protective clothing when we are in the sun or wear gloves when using harsh household cleaners, and we know to find shelter in times of inclement weather. Being exposed does not feel safe.

At times I felt that discernment was something I was not capable of, as I wandered in the aftermath of my husband's choices. For most of my life I had learned to be careful about the dangers of exposure, but this wilderness walk was quite unpredictable. I would often get caught off guard by a hidden emotion or unexpected circumstance. At one point I found myself at a crossroad. I had to face yet another fear: to boldly share my feelings and not hold back because of my protected heart. I had to risk being vulnerable again, to be willing to be exposed.

At this junction I had another difficult decision to make. Shall I remain stuck in fear or bravely move out? Was I willing to put my heart in harm's way and be completely honest with my husband, to expose myself to more pain? At first, brutal honesty was much easier because of the raw emotions that erupted on a minute-by-minute and then gradually day-by-day basis. But as the days and months went by, it became much more difficult for me to share my fears, my concerns or my thoughts after the initial heat of my rage subsided. I would struggle with asking my husband another question or telling him about my fears. Sometimes Rick would get frustrated. Again, the voice of my past would whisper, *"Don't open that door."* The emotional roller coaster ride of deciding to be courageous or to fall back into old behaviors was sometimes dizzying.

There was a tell-tale sign that let me know when I needed to ask a question; it would become quite apparent. My first clue would be a rapidly increasing heartbeat as a thought or question would enter my mind, and then even without realizing it, my body would go on autopilot. I would hold my breath, my "not wanting to feel" response would kick in, and within a few seconds I would begin the self-talk spankings. *"You do not need to ask that question, you already asked that before, what are you thinking?"* *"If you ask him that, then he will go back to that place visually and mentally in order to remember, and he will have to think of 'her' to answer that lame question."* *"If you tell him that you are struggling again with that detail, it will shame him once again and it will cause another setback, moving forward will take that much longer, just let it go."* On and on my arguments would go. My brain convincing my heart (or my heart convincing my brain) to avoid a conversation, afraid there would be more pain, more reconciling, and more heartache to follow.

Journal Entry, February 2, 2003
> *I am confused.*
> *How do I do this new life? How do I talk to Rick?*
> *If I say anything I mess up our night.*
> *If I don't say anything at all about my feelings and*
>   *hold them in I totally mess up our night.*
> *What am I supposed to do God? I need some*
>   *help here!*
> *How do I keep doing this?*
> *Help me!*

I noticed that, as my husband was discovering his bro-kenness from his childhood wounds, I would try to protect him from hurting any more. This was not a healthy way of dealing with my own aching heart. The self-talk allowed me to convince myself that I wasn't important enough to share how I felt or what I was going through. I learned the hard way that holding back was only creating more conflict, more emotional distress. I had to retrain my mind and my heart that I was important, that I mattered; I had to fight the negative thoughts.

After much aerobic activity in my mind, I came to realize that, in order for both of us to continue to heal, we had to be willing to be vulnerable. We had to take risks and be completely honest with each other, choos-ing to be as respectful as we could so as not to allow our defensive walls to be reconstructed. This was some-thing that we had not done in our past. Neither one of us felt that we could become that exposed; we did not feel safe with each other. We had built our sturdy emotional walls and blamed and denied our way through the first twenty-two years of our life together. But, with palpable apprehension, we began to practice sharing our honest feelings until we learned that being exposed with each other *was* safe. We were learning not to protect ourselves from the elements of the fear—fear of the past or fear of the unknown.

The Right Decision?

At times, discerning your situation can be quite difficult. During this season choose to be patient. Hang on a little longer. Dare to boldly share your true feelings, become willing to expose your heart. If you decide to risk being vulnerable and to courageously move out of your protective shelter, you will soon discover that you *are* capable of trusting your intuitions during this unstable time. Your emotions may feel unpredictable as you venture out, but strive to listen to the messages until they are clear. Your instincts may feel totally wrong and your ability to truly decipher what your head is saying and what your heart is feeling can be confusing and frightening. Trust your heart.

I know this seems irrational. You may be saying to yourself, "*But I followed my heart, and that is what got me into this mess.*" I understand; this was difficult for me to wrap my head around as well. However, I was extremely determined to move on—I did not want to stay immobilized in my pain. When I began to practice reading my journal entries out loud, I was able to hear what my heart was trying to tell me. Let me emphasize again, this took time. I would ask my Guide to help me to discern between the two.

When I decided to try to trust God with my wounded heart, I struggled often with my "where are you God" thoughts. I failed miserably time and again because of my trust issues with God as my Guide. I learned that the peace of mind I was searching for and pleading with God to help me with was not a one-time event.

I have known many people who have dared to say that, when you find God, all your troubles will go away. That is just not true! Life hurts, and as long as we are alive we will struggle with painful issues. In spite of my trust problem, I tried to allow God to guide me. I would ask God to give me peace in the moment, and I asked God to give me discernment in my uncertainty. It may not have come the very second that I asked, but I chose to believe that God cared deeply about me and wanted me to awaken from this nightmare. This wilderness journey was not his intention for my life, or yours, but he will not waste our pain either. You will come out of this more alive and free than ever before, if you will do the hard work. I found that my willingness to *try* to trust God, along with my writing and reading out loud, was instrumental in the healing of my wounded heart.

It had been quite some time since my counselor gave me her wise advice, "Follow your heart; you will then make the right decision." She was right, I listened; I heard. And I became more courageous as I moved on to the next leg of my wilderness journey.

Heart ready, trusting in God ...

Psalm 112:7b, *The Message*

Sometimes God seems so quiet!
However, when we see the way He works in lives imprisoned
by walls or circumstances, when we hear how faith
can shine through uncertainty,
we begin to catch a glimpse of the fruit of
patience that can grow out of the experience of suffering.

Billy Graham

The day came when the risk it took to remain
tight in the bud
was more painful than the risk it took to blossom.

Anais Nin

I will write myself into well-being.

Nancy Mair

❤ HEART WORK

Hopefully you have practiced getting alone by yourself often and have been listening with your heart. I suggest at this point in your journey that you take some time and get away from anything or anyone that may distract you. Once you have arranged it so you are completely alone, take out your notebook and read your written words out loud, starting from day one to the present. This exercise will assist your heart and mind. The discerning messages are there, waiting to be revealed.

Choose to listen to your Guide, and to your heart. They are what you must rely upon, as they will drive the flow and content of your journals. Continue with your journaling until complete healing has been attained. You may find that writing and reading your feelings out loud will be the means of finding peace of mind even beyond this nightmare, as you continue your journey through life.

12

CONSIDER THE RISKS

When we forgive evil we do not excuse it,
we do not tolerate it, we do not smother it.
We look the evil full in the face, call it what it is,
let its horror shock and stun and enrage us,
and only then do we forgive it.

Lewis B. Smedes

The Prison of Un-Forgiveness

Journal Entry, December 20, 2002
> *Forgiveness? How can I get to that place in my life?*
> *How can I forgive the one who betrayed my heart?*
> *I know I must get to this place of forgiveness; God*
> *help me!*
> *I know that I am in a prison of evil by hanging onto*
> *this anger, this contempt.*

> I know this is an important step in my healing, but
>   it needs to be real. Right?
> I must forgive those who sinned against me.
> How? How can I do this?
> What a burden, to be unforgiving towards those
>   who hurt me.
> Why do I want to hang on to the hate? How can
>   I truly let it go?
> I know in your time I will be able to forgive, I need
>   to be set free.
> Is this the last step of healing before I can move on?
> Oh God—I want so badly to move on—give me
>   what I need!
> You know my heart God. Guide me, please!
> Give me courage to do what you would have
>   me do.

Before I could even dare take the first steps toward learning to trust my husband, I had to visit a very dark and hostile place, the prison of unforgiveness. If I wanted to become free from the bondage of my husband's betrayal and the destruction that it caused, I had to be willing to crawl down into the dungeon of bitterness and resentment and face the effects of these emotions on my soul. If I did not confront them, then trust could never be possible. I would be a prisoner of animosity and disdain forever. Feelings of pride or superiority would become my prison guards.

Freedom from this hostile environment was my goal, but attaining this freedom could be risky; the heavy chains of fear would at times hold me down as I tried to break free. How could I forgive the lies, the shame, and the betrayal? Will I ever be able to forgive? Will it be too soon?

How do I know if I have forgiven him, or the other persons involved?

As a woman who grew up with the instruction that said, "If you do not forgive, then your own sins will not be forgiven," I wrestled with forgiveness as a part of my recovery. My conflict was not only with my own mind, but also with my religious convictions. This discovery presented me with many challenges I had to overcome before I could move on to restoring my life.

After much struggle with my need to forgive Rick, I realized as I had with every other step, that I had a decision to make. I had to decide if I wanted to think about forgiving my husband. Notice that I said, "think." Thinking for me was the very first step. I had to be willing to consider all the risks that forgiveness could involve. If I forgave, would it mean that my husband is off the hook, that life can go on as if none of this had happened? Would it mean that I was supposed to just put this all behind me, move on and forget the pain and destruction that this caused? What about all of my losses, my anger? I still have a right to be angry, don't I?

The chains would tighten as I struggled in my mind. The unknowns created fear and panic. Was my heart deceiving me?

Heart Messages

So how do you listen to your heart regarding forgiveness when in your mind there is so much confusion?

You must never rush forgiveness. Forgiving the offender too soon can be an escape strategy to avoid the pain of not wanting to confront the issues that have invaded your world. Sooner or later, an event will trigger the unprocessed pain; you will have to face it one day. On the other hand, waiting too long to begin the passage to forgiveness can create a hard, callused heart that refuses to feel or risk loving again. Disdain and contempt will sneak up on you like a vicious animal, waiting to pounce on you while you navigate towards a new life. You risk beginning to feel superior and hard of heart. This is where bitterness and resentment creeps in. If these are permitted to grow and fester, they will become very destructive to your health and *all* your relationships. If you decide to stay self-protected and are unwilling to release the chains of unforgiveness, your heart will atrophy and will slowly shrivel up and die.

Dr. Dan B. Allender makes an important point in the book *Bold Love* regarding forgiveness and repentance. He writes:

> Forgiveness involves a heart that cancels the debt but does not lend new money until repentance occurs. A forgiving heart opens the door to any who knock. But entry into the home (that is the heart) does not occur until the muddy shoes and dirty coat have been taken off. The offender must repent if true intimacy and reconciliation are ever to take place. That means that cheap forgiveness—peace at any cost that sacrifices honesty, integrity, and passion-is not true forgiveness. [4]

Once you have made your decision to think about forgiveness and have calculated the costs, you then begin the very long process of forgiving the offender and the offense.

The Price You Pay

Remember this: *forgiving is not a feeling.* If you wait to feel forgiving, or if you want to feel the feeling of forgiveness, you will never get there. Freedom from your own prison of resentment is what will be gained, not a feeling.

Mark Twain accurately observed, "Forgiveness is the fragrance the violet sheds on the heel that has crushed it." Read that again, slowly.

We have been crushed; our hearts have been trampled on and broken. Our lives have been torn into tiny fragments of rejection, shame, despair, and desolation. The wounded heart cries out, it screams of being robbed, violated, and dishonored by someone we thought we knew, trusted, and believed would never betray the vows we made.

I remember my heart hurting so severely it literally felt as if someone had put my soft, fragile organ in a vise and was slowly squeezing the life out of it. There would be no relief from the agony that I bore. I would scream out to God, "When, when will my heart stop hurting?" That question never seemed to be answered.

Journal Entry, January 3, 2003
A new year, a rough start for me.
God, when will I heal?
When will my heart stop hurting?
When will I not feel like such a fool?
Why didn't I see this coming?
Years, years of memories that don't really mean
anything to me right now.
What a waste!

I feel so alone, so insecure.

I feel afraid.

God, help me now!

Help me not to feel so afraid.

I know that you are with me.

BUT GOD!!! I NEED SOME RELIEF!!!

I feel such torment in my brain. My body shakes, my mind is numb.

Please give me something to help with this pain.

I look at pictures now, the latest ones of the two of us.

I see a peace in Rick's eyes that was not there before.

I am so happy for him, but the roles have been reversed.

Now, I am not present, I am not all there.

My eyes are empty. My soul is void of life.

I cannot give myself fully to my husband.

My heart is heavy almost all of the time.

I have moments that are good, but they are getting farther and farther apart. Why?

I feel such a loss, and yet I have gained so much.

When will I be done with this?

All I ever wanted was to be loved and to love.

Now I am loved, but I can't love as deeply as I did before.

Will I get my love back? Will I?

Oh God, please help me!

Will I always have this pain in my life?

God! I need you to show yourself to me today.

I need your security.

I need your peace.
Please help me today.
I feel so alone.

As you move through this very difficult phase of thinking about and then deciding to forgive, remember; remember that it will not happen overnight. You will be processing your anger and sadness for a very long time. Down the road you will think that you have forgiven, and then out of nowhere, emotions will erupt. You may find a photo that was taken on your anniversary or at a special event, and the memory of that day brings tears to your eyes and the blood rushes to your face as you feel the betrayal all over again. If your favorite love song comes on the radio and you can no longer sing along with the lyrics, the torment of the betrayal floods your soul once more. You feel buried alive again in uncontrollable grief and unresolved anger.

Journal Entry, January 28, 2003
> *I was listening to an old song today, one that I had enjoyed years before. As I listened I was thinking about Rick, remembering how I felt years ago. I don't have those same feelings now.*
> *I feel there is a big hole in my heart—in my love for Rick right now.*
> *What does that mean?*
> *Is it gone forever?*
> *When I think of how much I loved Rick—how much I adored him—I become so sad.*

*Because of my tower (my walls), I could never let
him know just how much I loved him.*

*So many losses. When will I stop mourning what
I lost?*

I wish I could love Rick like I did before.

My heart aches as I write that.

*I feel as if the world around me is going back to
normal, but my heart is still bleeding.*

*I am not sure what I am to do with these
feelings.*

Everyday my heart hurts!

*Everyday I ache for my losses—what I could have
had!*

*Yes, I do have a glimmer of hope once in awhile,
but I am still hurting.*

*What do I do with this? I am angry and I feel the
anger growing.*

*I know Rick loves me, but I can't love him the way
I use to.*

Oh, God help me!

*I feel like I am in a mucky pond and my feet are
stuck. I can't pull them out. I feel so stuck in all
parts of my life right now.*

I am so stuck.

Have I lost my love forever?

Journal Entry, April 25, 2003

Grief.

*My sorrow overwhelms me. My sobbing
consumes me.*

I have lost heart; I am hollow inside.

I focus on my losses.

Why? Why do I stare down the many losses?
I am mourning again—deep groans of pain
*   and loss.*
I feel as if I am sitting opposite of a tomb.
Here I sit, staring at a tomb of death. My marriage
*   is dead.*
My dreams are dead, and my trust is dead.
Death of a life I knew.
What I had before is gone, forever.
Dead. Gone.
Death delivers such a sting.
Is there no relief?
Who am I? Who was my husband?
Betrayal.
How can you describe the pain of betrayal?

When I chose to begin the process of forgiving my husband, I was agreeing to live with the consequences of his wrongdoing. When I decided to engage the process of forgiveness, I knew that there would be a price for the transgression that I was forgiving. I was already living with those consequences; there was no other path to tread.

There were days that I had to will myself to forgive, again and again. It was hard at times, but I knew this act of choosing to forgive was another phase of this journey that would lead me to True North—my awakening, my way out of this wilderness.

I was moving forward, gradually. My crooked and narrow trail was expanding. The thick and suffocating forest canopy was thinning, allowing the sun to break through and shed light into the darkness. I could feel deep within my being that my wounds were healing. As I chose the path of forgiveness, slowly, step-by-step, my heart began to heal.

Keep on your path towards freedom. There will be days when you will trip over the small stones or ruts of "How could he/she do this to me?" thoughts. The feelings of never trusting again are heavy and cumbersome as you try to remove the fallen debris that comes across your trail. At times it may feel as if you will never make it through the thick brambles of anger and fear. This portion of the mountainous terrain will take a very long time, so please do not believe the lies that batter your weary mind as you continue this journey—the lies that murmur, "If only you would have_____," or "Why didn't you_____?" You can get through this most difficult period; keep moving forward to find the clearing. It is out there, I promise.

Painful Observations

I trudged along in the forgiveness phase of my journey, guarding my heart for quite some time. One day fused gradually into the next, and then it happened. I began to understand just a bit of a world that I could not have comprehended just months before. Some of the answers to my tormenting questions of how could my husband blatantly disregard weddings vows, moral values, and family commitments for a fling of the flesh became clearer. Eventually I began to feel sorry for him and the other persons involved. My heart began to feel sadness for the pain in their pasts that caused them to feel that they had to participate in such damaging behaviors. As I courageously stepped out and allowed my heart to risk being exposed once again, I could almost tangibly feel the armor that protected my fragile heart slowly begin to melt.

Trying to understand my husband's behavior was painfully brutal at times. During this challenging time, I had to become a bystander and helplessly watch my oldest son Caleb choose for a time to destroy his life with drug addiction. As I agonized over my son's choices, I wondered, *"How can I survive the onslaught of the emotional despair of my husband's unfaithfulness and at the same time deal with the anguish of a son who is killing himself with drugs?"* I made the decision that I could survive this nightmare and, if I chose to do so, I could learn from my son's behavior. As I stood on the outside looking in on Caleb's life, I discovered the roots of his actions. In spite of wishing I did not have to learn these lessons in this way, I began to understand why a person would make life-altering decisions that would devastate a family.

My son's addictive behavior taught me that, when people are profoundly wounded from past experiences, they are in such emotional pain that they will do anything to numb out, to not feel. Or, they will do whatever they can just to feel something extreme because the pain and fear are so prevalent.

Many people try to fill the giant hole in their soul by becoming entangled in an adulterous relationship to give them a feeling or rush, even if it is just for that moment. If they have not learned to be completely numb from the feelings about their behavior, then they are full of shame because of their actions; thus the cycle begins again. When they feel shame, they desperately don't want to feel that, so they begin to act out and the downward spiral starts all over, acting out to feel better, repeating this destructive behavior over and over again.

As I allowed myself to stand back and separate myself from my nightmare, I began to grasp the reasons for Rick's unfaithfulness, as well as our son's drug use. Both were in response to a desperate search to fill a void in their broken lives. They either needed to numb themselves because they hurt so badly, or they were wanting to feel something to help deaden their pain.

It is extremely important for you, the faithful, to work on your own issues and discover your own broken parts so that you can respond appropriately as you begin to understand why your spouse acted out. Please hear me here; this process will take time. When you get to this place in your journey of restoration, when you are genuinely concerned for the one who has hurt you and sincerely want them to get well, you will be able honestly to say you have forgiven them for what they have done. Then you will know you are free. There is nothing in this world but our willingness to forgive that frees us from our prison of anger, resentment, and fear.

Purple Beauties

Two years after my husband's confession, a truly remarkable event occurred. Something that we never thought would ever happen to us surprisingly did. My husband was asked to take an assistant position in a church in Washington State. In that community, with the guidance of a lead pastor and a congregation, we would continue with our recovery, no longer alone. During our time there, as I continued to move forward in my healing, the prison chains of anger and fear began to fall off. I had truly embraced the freedom of forgiveness.

The first summer in our new home I noticed that the previous owner had planted a few violets in the yard. By the end of the first summer, the purple beauties overran my garden. I was amazed at how sturdy they were. They could be mowed, trampled, torn, and sprayed; but nothing would deter their growth and their ability to reseed and spread. I could not get rid of them. The following year as I was trying to uproot some unruly violets that had taken over an area in my patio, I felt God nudge me and say, *"I have given these violets to you as a reminder of your willingness to forgive. Once you have forgiven, there is no getting rid of the freedom that you receive. These purple gifts are for you to remember what it cost to get to this place in your life. Enjoy!"*

Mark Twain was right about forgiveness. The fragrance that is squeezed from our crushed lives can be the most intoxicating aroma—of freedom! Yes, we have been crushed; but our hearts can explode with the scent of trampled violets! It is well worth the cost. But this, too, will take a long time to achieve. Take the time to consider the costs and the risks and then slowly decide to move forward with the process of forgiveness.

Journal Entry, January 30, 2005

> *I thought that I had forgiven my husband.*
> *In my mind I had gone through every step of forgiving.*
> *I prayed, I wrote letters, I pleaded with God.*
> *I even went as far as having pity for the ones who betrayed me.*
> *But there was still a torment in my mind daily.*
> *I felt like I was holding Rick hostage.*
> *I struggled letting go of the past.*
> *All this time I thought I had forgiven him.*
> *I understand now; forgiveness is a process.*
> *I thought as time went by it would just happen on its own.*
> *It did not.*
> *I realize after more heart work that I had forgiven my husband with my mind, but not my heart.*
> *I am finally there!*
> *I AM FREE!*
> *Free from the bondage of an unforgiving heart.*
> *I am free, and now Rick is free as well!*
> *Thank you God for guiding my life once again.*
> *Now I can live.*
> *I AM FREE!*

Forgiveness is a rebirth of hope,
a reorganization of thought,
and a reconstruction of dreams.
Once forgiving begins, dreams can be rebuilt.
When forgiving is complete,
meaning has been extracted from the worst of experiences
and used to create a new set of moral rules and a new
interpretation of life's events.

Beverly Flanigan

True forgiveness is a very strong and clean
and masculine virtue.
There is a counterfeit forgiveness, which is
unworthy of the name.
It is full of "peradventures." It moves with reluctance, it offers
with averted face, it takes back with one hand what it
gives with the other ...
It forgives, but it "can never trust again."...
What kind of forgiveness it this?

John Henry Jowett

Forgiveness is the answer to a child's dream of a miracle
by which what is broken is made whole again,
what is soiled is again made clean.

Dag Hammarskjöld

♥ HEART WORK

Did you believe prior to this nightmare that the act of forgiving was a one-time event? Where are you on the forgiveness path? Have you calculated the cost of forgiving your spouse and the other person involved with the betrayal?

Whether you have stayed with your spouse or not, do you find yourself holding the betrayer hostage with punishing behaviors or statements? Do you obsess with scenarios in your mind of how you could have "caught the two of them," letting the scenes play over and over in your mind? Or, if you did catch your spouse in the act, do you reprimand yourself for your reactive behaviors? This is all part of the process of facing the brutal act of infidelity as you journey toward forgiveness. Be kind to yourself as you continue through this difficult and lengthy phase. However, do not allow yourself to linger overlong in this phase; be willing to push through it. Have conversations with your Guide; stay connected with your counselor and work diligently on your own issues.

> *Remember, do not rush this part of your journey. Healing will come as you continue to process your feelings appropriately. You will pass through this time to find the healing that your heart desires.*

13

LOOK FOR A CLEARING

*"Confusion is the dust raised by the feet of the Devil,
calculated to cloud your vision and blind your eyes ...*

Frances J. Roberts

Journal Entry, November 23, 2002

> *The Lord says, forget what happened before
> and do not think about the past.
> Look at the new thing that I am going to do.
> It's already happening.
> Don't you see it?*

Isaiah 43:19, *NCV*

*I have questions for you God!
What do you mean by these words?
It's 2:30 A.M. I can't sleep. Why? What is going on
in my head?*

My eyes burn—they sting so badly.

It's such a burden to keep them open and yet, I cannot sleep.

I guess I am processing again.

Does nothing of my past matter?

How can I not go back and look at my past?

How can I not wonder about so many things, and to read that it doesn't matter?

Do the memories, the vacations, the Holidays, or birthdays not matter?

The same disconnected husband, the same man all those years who didn't want to be married to me, and I am to forget it all?!!

So what did matter? If none of the past matters, what was my past?

This is so very confusing.

How could I be intimate with a man who I could not be intimate with?

I blamed myself for twenty-two years; it was my fault our marriage wasn't working.

I was the sick one—so Rick told me over and over.

Please God, if it does not matter to you, then help me let it go.

Oh, I need wisdom right now!

How could I be vulnerable with someone who didn't respect me or love me?

All those years of suffering, trying to figure it out, trying to be loved—it was so hard.

This does not matter?!!

How can I forget the past?

From day one, nothing was clear. Nothing made sense. My husband's infidelity was not just a betrayal of our marriage. That alone would have been difficult to bear, but my own self-interrogations about my past would haunt me for months on end. *"What had been real in our relationship and what was not?"* I would wrestle for a long time with how I could have been so foolish not to pay attention to the red flags. *"Why did I not see the signs? What made my husband disregard our wedding vows?" "Who is this stranger that lived in my house?" "How could my husband abandon our family, and our life—for what?"*

I could not comprehend how a man could stand in front of a congregation and teach about the trap of adultery and then fall so foolishly into the snare of this insidious transgression. My mind would be confused and tormented on a daily basis. *"Why couldn't he say no to the temptations that were challenging him? Couldn't he have prayed harder, tried harder, or at the least talked to me about his struggles?"*

The battery of questions seemed endless. I needed clarity; I needed to understand so I could begin to make sense of this mess. I needed help.

During the early days of our recovery, our counselor said to me, "Patti, the little boy in Rick caused this to happen. It does not excuse the man; what Rick did was wrong, but the little boy inside him made it happen."

When my counselor made that shocking statement I sat on her couch in total disbelief and confusion. *"How could a little boy cause this to happen? My husband is a grown man, a very strong-willed man. How could anyone make him do anything?"*

Journal Entry, October 31, 2002

> *You abused my mind. Will I ever understand?*
>
> *So, there is supposed to be a wounded little boy in there?*
>
> *BUT, you are a man and you could have said "NO."*
>
> *When will all this make sense?*
>
> *You could have been a stand-up man.*
>
> *You could have told me you were struggling, instead of telling me that I was the one who had problems.*
>
> *Couldn't we have worked it out?*
>
> *I guess I am a little late in that request.*
>
> *I hurt so badly. How long will I have to suffer?*
>
> *Thirty-seven years is a long time God to live in pain, confusion, turmoil, tragedy.*
>
> *When will it be over? When I die?*

The Dust Settles

Prior to Rick's confession, I had spent quite a bit of time in counseling. For years Rick had insisted that our marriage was not working because I was the broken one, so I decided that I had better figure out what was wrong with me. I worked very hard on my past issues, and as a result I began to understand and take hold of the idea that childhood wounds follow us into the present. My early emotional injuries did influence certain unhealthy choices and actions.

I discovered that, because of my father's own pain over my mother's abandonment of him and our family, he was incapable of loving me the way a young girl desperately needed. As a result of the actions of both my mother and father, I was destined to live out my life wanting desperately to be loved. Because of my trust issues, I subconsciously protected myself and would not allow anyone to get too close for fear that they would abandon me. If I exposed my fragile heart, they might reject me. I lived a self-fulfilling prophecy; the thing that I feared the most became my reality. My childhood belief system, combined with the penetrating message "don't open doors" from the earlier motel event, set me up to develop behaviors that would damage both me and my family. My emotions were protected in a strong tower; the fortified walls were tall and very thick. A frightened, isolated, abandoned little girl crafted all of this thinking.

Even though I had a couple of years of therapy behind me and was able to understand some of the psychological effects of how a broken childhood can create unhealthy and even irrational behaviors, I was not able to apply the discovery of my damaged belief system from my childhood to my husband's unfaithfulness. I could not for the life of me grasp how the wounds from his childhood would cause him to do something so devastating to others and to himself. I was stuck in my own pain, which made it impossible at first to understand how the belief system of the little boy, inside of the man, could allow something so immoral and destructive. It would take months of wrestling with such thoughts and ideas before I could get a clear understanding.

Journal Entry, November 22, 2002
> *When will the whys go away?*
> *When will I be able to truly grasp that there is a*
> *   little boy inside of Rick?*
> *When will I believe it wasn't about sex?*
> *When will I stop getting visuals of them together?*

When will I feel secure about my own body?
Help me God. Help me when I go to those places
  in my mind.
PLEASE, PLEASE. PLEASE, I beg you to show me,
  teach me, heal me.
PLEASE, PLEASE, PLEASE!
At what point does the man, not the little boy have
  responsibility in all of this?

Paralyzing Reflections

I struggled and struggled to comprehend how a wounded boy could be trapped inside of a grown man. Then one day, after much wrestling with my heart and mind, I began to see a clearing. It was still way off in the distance. It was a small sliver of light, but it was enough to give me the clarity that I needed at that time. During the tumultuous days prior to my husband's confession and during the aftermath of his disclosure, we had been dealing with a most complicated and painful situation with one of our sons.

Early one morning, a few months before Rick's disclosure, our son walked into our bedroom as I was getting ready for work and very nonchalantly said, "Mom, I was molested by a babysitter when I was a little boy." I thought that he was making a joke, and I said that this was not something to tease about. He responded in a weak and vulnerable tone, "I am not joking, Mom."

As I stood paralyzed facing my reflection in the bathroom mirror, the look of horror stared back at me. My head instantly became fuzzy. I tried to control the dizzy waves of nausea that now consumed me. As the blood left my face, I had the sensation that life as a mother as I had known it would never be the same again. The room was spinning; I felt out of control. I heard my mind scream, *"No! This cannot be happening to us! How could this have happened?"*

I pulled myself together the best I could and asked (holding my breath), "Do you remember who did this to you? " He said, "Yes," and the story rolled out to our shock and horror. The next few months brought some of our most difficult days, as we tried to make sense of what had happened.

The rapid succession of events that followed our son's revelation would be overwhelming and emotionally exhausting, crushing our ability to trust in the legal system. We survived the painful police interrogation process. We were angry and stunned when we learned that the seven-year statute of limitation period had passed and that the sitter denied the accusations. Charges could not be brought. We were stuck with multiplied emotional distress.

Once all of the police formalities were settled, our son was able to begin working on the emotional trauma that had plagued his mind for years. The counselors began unraveling the reasons behind his extremely compulsive activities, his boundary-less behaviors, and his insatiable need for attention.

I tell you this very painful part of my life to let you know that, as I began to deal with the emotional trauma of my son's childhood wounds, and as I provided patient guidance to help him learn how to rebuild the boundaries that had been violated, some things became very clear. I began to see how my husband, a grown man, had gone through his whole adult life with the dark secret of his own sexual abuse locked inside since he was a young boy. I began to understand why

Rick could "act out" with behaviors that were so damaging and wounding. Digging into Rick's past allowed us to uncover some important facts. This information would help answer some of the nagging "why" questions.

Striving for Clarity

When Rick was four years old, his father became very ill and needed to live in as stress-free environment as possible. After major surgery, the doctor recommended that his father move to the Arizona desert to recover. Because of the stress factor, Rick and his younger brother went to stay with relatives in California, and his older sister lived with another family member in Oregon. Rick's father and mother moved to the desert and lived in a fourteen-foot travel trailer for four months. Eventually the family would be reunited and would continue to live in the small, cramped trailer for a few more months until their father was well enough to return to their home in Oregon. But he never fully recovered, and consequently he was incapable of being the father that Rick desperately needed. Every year that went by, the unspoken fear persisted that his father was dying. With his weakened immune system and fear of getting sick again, Rick's father could not spend quality time with his children. This young family learned to live in a home with an emotionally disconnected and sick dad.

Without the guidance of a father, Rick would learn to play sports, fish, hunt, and do most things by himself. In reality, Rick learned to live much of life all by himself. Those years with a virtually absent father left gaping wounds. A young boy is not capable of understanding the complexities of such situations, so the message goes on the belief board like this: "I must not be good enough to be loved by my dad." This false belief would create in Rick an insatiable need to be loved by someone, especially a man who could provide love, attention and affirmation.

Rick's sixth-grade teacher quickly picked up on Rick's father-wound and began spending inappropriate time with him, eventually sexually molesting Rick, shattering his already confused mind and validating his inaccurate belief system. Rick did not have the mental capacity or recourses to process the teacher's sexual advances. Hurt people hurt people, and so the cycle would continue.

Deep emotional wounds are inevitable when you combine a teacher's sexual exploitation, Rick's pre-school separation from the family and his emotionally absent and physically ill father. To complicate the scenario even more, Rick's well-intentioned mother tried to compensate for the relational disconnect with his father. In Rick's desperate search for love and attention, it's not surprising that a relationally-hungry time bomb was ticking within him, ready to detonate.

Years after this catastrophic event of sexual abuse, the bomb did explode. The devastation that followed would wound many trusting people. The aftershocks would last for years. Many church members, friends, and family would question Rick's role as husband, father, spiritual leader, and friend. Some still do.

Boundaries Broken

When a child is sexually abused, one of the resulting emotional wounds is the inability to keep appropriate boundaries. The trauma robs the child of the ability to distinguish where he or she ends, and someone else begins.

I now understood why my son had such difficulty learning that "No" meant no. The damage that is inflicted on a child during and after the abuse undermines the developing "belief" system. To these abused children boundaries mean nothing. These shattered little boys and girls live their lives fearing adults and authority figures. This belief system may cause children to violate boundaries of other children, leaving them feeling ashamed and unlovable as they multiply the secrets of their experiences. Over time, the wounded child lives on in the interior core of the adult and will do just about anything to try to fill the unquenchable need to be loved and affirmed. The inner voices are persistent and convincing.

I remember the day when I looked deep into Rick's eyes and told him that I was still having difficulty understanding how a boy could possibly have so much power over a grown man's behavior. Since I learn things visually, Rick drew me a simple sketch to try to show me what he had discovered about his childhood belief system and how he finally understood the "whys" of his behavior. With his simply-drawn stick figure, Rick was able to explain how a little child does have the ability to continue to speak into an adult's life. The inner child will continue to have a voice until the survivor adult (the adult who is trying to survive the abuse or abuses) is willing to do the complex and difficult work of processing through the painful issues of the past.

Rick explained to me that the survivor adult would do anything to prove to the fear-driven child inside that he/she is lovable, that he/she is not flawed or repulsive. The survival instinct of the wounded adult (the survivor adult) easily falls into the trap with other wounded women or men with similar survivor adult "child voices" inside. The cycle repeats over and over until the healthy adult does the work of re-parenting and begins speaking healing messages to the frightened, wounded inner child.

The Message is Loud and Clear

Children believe that they caused their own abuse, or that they should have stopped it from happening. A child under twelve will often think, "What did I do to make this happen?" That leads to a belief statement which, if left unchallenged, becomes a key part of the child's belief system, and a sense of toxic shame is given birth. Unlike healthy shame, which feels remorse for inappropriate behavior, this toxic thinking causes the children to believe that they must be flawed if such a horrible thing happened to them. It's not so much shame for what they have done; they feel shame for who they are. And with that shame comes a strong desire to hide and never be found out. They also believe that if they tell anyone, no one will believe them, or that family members will be hurt (if the abuser used threats to silence the victim). My son's counselor told me that some little boys who are molested struggle with the fact that the acts used upon them felt good, thus baffling them even more. Sometimes a child will realize only much later that the episode was abuse.

Once this distorted belief system has been set up, the survivor adult will do everything to prove to their inner child that the fear messages from the belief system are not correct. For example, when a man inadvertently gets the attention of a woman, the survivor adult may subconsciously say to the inner child, "See, you are important, you don't have to be afraid, she likes you, she thinks you are funny." Or the inner voice may say something like, "See you're not so flawed; you are loveable."

The survivor adult may strive to override an inadequacy message by working more than what is required, in order to get the approval of the boss and co-workers, or to get praise from a disconnected, workaholic mother or father. Survivor adults are constantly trying to prove to their inner child that they are worthy or valuable. The response is the same. The voices have been screaming at them for years to prove to their broken selves: "I am worthy, I am not flawed! See?"

I've seen the other side of that coin too. Some abused children will grow up believing that they are repulsive because of what happened to them. They will feel a need to make sure no one ever finds them attractive again. Many survivors eat themselves to obesity to prove to their inner child, "*See you are right, you are repulsive, no one will want to touch you again, you are safe now.*"

You may have had a *Leave It to Beaver* childhood and today's wounds may be a direct result of your spouse's choices; but this I do know, there are broken parts in your life, too, that need to be mended. I truly believe that all of us have a message written on our belief system boards and we wear it across our inner core. The message may not be as debilitating as mine, "*You are a bad person if you open that door.*" The message may be as subtle as "*It's always your fault,*" because you accidentally left the front door open when you were a five year old and your pet dog was run over by a passing car. You were scolded and told that it was your fault, and you have carried that imprinted message with you forever. When a discouraging or threatening life event arises, your inner child voice screams at you loud and clear, "*It's always your fault! You should have_____.*" Intended or not, our parents, teachers, coaches or peers have the ability to leave lasting impressions on our fragile young minds that eventually end up on our inner belief system boards.

Over the last several years my husband and I have had the opportunity to share our story with many who ask. I am amazed at how, in the beginning of the conversation, they have no idea that each one of us carries a message board from our youth that informs what we currently think about ourselves. As we continue to dig deeper into their lives, their stories are revealed and they can trace the history of their shame-based belief system boards.

Consider this anonymous case of unintentional identity messages. An eleven-year old boy walks a pretty girl home from school and at the door he asks her mother if he can stay and play with her daughter. The mother responds, "A boy like you will never play with a girl like this." The imprinted message on this young boy's identity board, *"I am not good enough,"* is followed by the adult survivor message, *"I need to outperform everyone's expectations to prove that I am worthy."* This message crushed the young boy, shaped how he felt about himself and began to influence how he would relate to women for the next fifty years. The end result: the young man grew up hungry for commendation in every aspect of his life. He worked for proofs of his worth. He received many accolades for his high achievements from his adoring father, his mother, and his peers in the work place. Upon retirement and after the deaths of his mother and father, this respected man had no one to sing his praises or to influence that fragile belief from his childhood. His wife was not his "cheerleader." She was not capable of filling his insatiable need for admiration. So, because his childhood message screamed louder than mature reasoning, he proceeded to pay for his needed approval by hiring women to adore him. Because of his generosity and his large bank account, this behavior intensified. These broken women had never satisfied their unquenchable longings either. So, a highly intelligent, greatly honored community leader ended up paying money to replace the admiration and affirmations that he lost when he retired and his parents died. His choices triggered a catastrophic marital disaster, leaving his retirement account empty and many people struggling to understand how a man, who said he loved God, adored his wife and taught a Sunday-school class could ever turn his life in such a direction.

Childhood messages are powerful. They can control all aspects of our lives. Until we do the hard work of uncovering these messages, we will continue to struggle in our relationships. When the survivor adult stops trying to soothe the fear messages of the inner child, it is an indication that a healthy adult is emerging. It is at this point that the healthy adult can begin to re-parent the inner child and set the inner child free.

I know not all who commit adultery were sexually molested. What I have found, however, is that past wounds are imprinted in the mind of the betrayers. These wounded adults will end up shattering their lives and the lives of those that they love in one way or another.

Adultery may not be the thing that causes destruction; it could be a gambling addiction, or an alcohol addiction. I know a man who buys every newspaper that he can get his hands on and reads every page, everyday, while watching the news on television, completely neglecting his responsibilities as a husband and father. No one was allowed to talk to him while he obsessed with his numbing behavior. What message did he as a young boy write on his self-identity board?

An over-demanding, abusive father or a neglectful, "I don't give a rip" dad or mother can create messages that might make an adult search for someone other than their spouse to lavish attention and love on the wounded inner child. Or, it is possible that a mother may overcompensate for the father's neglect or addiction by becoming excessively controlling or overly affectionate, showering admiration and praise on the child—thus sending the emerging adult on a search to fill an unquenchable need for recognition and the deficit in father direction.

I am sorry that our son had to go through such a dreadful ordeal as a young boy. My heart breaks for him and all the children who have been subjected to such atrocities. I believe that, because of my son's sexual abuse and his struggle to wellness, I was able to move forward in the healing of my own damaged emotions and learn to accept the whys and hows of my husband's unfaithfulness.

Now I could understand the meaning of my nighttime messenger from many months before, *"You don't abandon little boys; you hold them, you love them; you do not leave them."* I had to be willing to love the broken little boy trapped inside my husband. In doing so, I was able to be patient and supportive as he rewrote the broken messages from his wounded past.

The dust cloud of doubt and confusion cleared. I could finally see.

Striving for understanding was a very important part of my ability to recover from the emotional pain of infidelity. I had to fight for this part of my healing. I struggled against my mind. The *"How could he do this?"* tape played over and over in my head. I fought against physical limitations from sleepless nights and mind-fogged days. I was in opposition to well-intended people who tried to sway my thinking and made me at times question all things regarding my choices, my future and my new life.

I urge you to continue with your striving until you have the understanding you need. Whether you had a life that has given you false messaging or the brokenness of your marriage was your first trauma, strive for clarity—clarity of your spouse's behavior and your own. You will then be able to move closer to your healing and recovery from your spouse's betrayal.

More Understanding

After the initial shock of my husband's betrayal began to wane, I felt I was on a mission to try to understand how anyone could possibly fall into the trap of infidelity. Why do men and women choose to have a secret life apart from their own families? Why do they risk everything for a fling with a stranger, a friend, or a coworker? I set out to learn as much as I could about infidelity. I felt that I needed to try to understand the reasons that someone would choose to have an affair. After hours and hours of reading various articles and research papers that have been written on this topic, I started gathering the results.

There are multiple reasons that a person will choose to have an affair. Current research on sexual behaviors shows that some men, out of fear of getting too close to their wives, will be unfaithful. There are also the entitled adulterers. These people, mostly men, are not necessarily unhappy in their marriages, but if they see an attractive woman and she appears to be interested, they initiate a sexual contact. For these unrestrained people, it is like walking into a restaurant and seeing a slice of strawberry pie on the lunch menu. The pie looks delicious, probably smells great, but they are not hungry. However, they will order and eat the strawberry pie anyway.

There are some women who live with an emotionally distant husband; these women may cheat because they are lonely and are feeling abandoned by their spouses. She desires intimacy and will succumb to that longing by finding another man's willing conversation and touch. In most cases the marriage is already in trouble, which leaves the woman quite vulnerable to the above-mentioned men. Coworkers and spousal best-friend affairs often fall into this category of adulterers.

There are men and some women who are predatory adulterers. These people most likely have a self-centered personality; they are quite confident and charming with their enticements. In order to satiate their inflated egos, they believe they must prove to the opposite sex that they are gifts to humankind. The media is never shy about exploiting this type of adulterer, as we have witnessed often in the past.

Being a sex addict is another possible reason for a person to fall into the trap of infidelity. These men and women have an intense sexual appetite or an obsession with sex. They will engage in risky behaviors, most often blaming their spouses for their problems and denying that their behaviors are of any consequence. Compulsive masturbation, extra marital affairs, one-night stands, consistent use of porn, phone sex, and the use of prostitutes are often the result of this addictive behavior.

In 2005, the *Journal of Marital and Family Therapy* conducted an exhaustive study. Polls were taken from twenty-six countries around the world. Researchers were not able to clarify why people would engage in an extra marital relationship. They wondered why high profile people with much to lose and those who have deep religious convictions still participated in the behavior. Once the data was compiled, two questions asked by the researchers were analyzed: "How does the undesirable behavior become desirable?" and "How do people weigh the decision against the extreme cost?"[5] The final result was simply that more research needs to be done in order to understand why a person would engage is such morally inappropriate behaviors.

Another study revealed that Americans are becoming more intolerant of extramarital relationships. The National Science Foundation's Longitudinal General Social Survey found in 2006 that 80.6 percent of Americans said that infidelity is always wrong.[6] Yet, men and women continue to break their wedding vows. Many theories and statistics are out there as to why a person would have an affair. Intelligent, well-intended people have come out with many hypotheses. Isn't it interesting that a person can have so much information but still does not find the answers to the whys of infidelity? It has been the same old reasons for years and years with the same outcomes, and yet men and women continue to participate in this devastating behavior. Perhaps they are not asking the right questions.

The Reasons Behind The Reasons

I believe, after having survived infidelity with my marriage intact and having many difficult conversations with my husband, and later having the opportunity to dialogue with both spouses and adulterers, wounds of the past are the main contributors to infidelity. Discussions with professionals in behavioral psychology have confirmed my findings. Secular studies have been completed and published with hundreds of men and woman participating in polls that reveal some very important facts. But I believe

that the deep wounds of our past, either by abandonment issues, physical and/or sexual abuse, or other childhood wounds create a belief system that often leaves an
intense fear of intimacy. These unprocessed emotional
injuries will ultimately impair our ability to bond with our
marriage partners.

Drug addiction, food addictions, and other vices are
compensations for such abuses as well. We need relief
from the pain, so we do whatever we can to numb our
senses. We have all done this "numbing out"—with food,
TV, gardening, spending, etc. Whatever we do to numb
or medicate only creates more emptiness, fear, and aloneness. Confusion, emotional pain and shame are the end
results.

As I have attempted to learn as much as I could about the
reasons a person commits adultery, I have become increas-
ingly amazed by the lack of knowledge in the Christian
community on this issue. Or maybe they have put blinders
on because so many of our Christian leaders are filled with
shame themselves and have nowhere to go to talk about
their own secret addictions and their broken, shattered
lives. Or could it be that society has defined the reasons for
infidelity, and the Christian community has adopted their
explanations without question?

I recently listened to a podcast on the Internet. Three
well-respected pastors were sharing their thoughts and
experiences on how to restore a person in ministry who had
had a moral failure. Even with their thirty years of ministry,
with all of their collective knowledge, they did not touch on
the issue of the early-life brokenness in the one who failed
morally. They were convinced that those who failed by sexual

immorality did so because they simply had unconfessed sin in their lives. I was a bit shocked, needless to say.

That is just one more reason why I feel we must get out to the world the message that wounds of the past can cause a person to become vulnerable to breaking their wedding vows. It's not always just a fling, or that they need more sex, or a person has caught their eye. It may not have anything to do with whether or not someone is unfulfilled in his or her current relationship. It is definitely *not* about whether a woman is pretty enough or sexy enough, and it is not as simple as an unconfessed sin. It is much deeper than that. There is more to understand so that the healing can begin. Until our society, both secular and Christian, embraces the deeper issues of adultery and decides to reject the mindset that "men will be men" and "women are unhappy in their relationships," the cycles will continue and more and more families will be traumatized.

Forgetting? Not Possible

I may not ever be able to forget the past, but I can choose to look forward to a better, healthier future with my husband. I groped blindly at first, stumbled, fell, and nursed my wounds as I continued on my journey. Then one day my path became clearer. I could see that there was a new thing happening; it just took time to see it fully. I worked very hard to find clarity for my new life. I pray as you strive for understanding of your own story and as you continue to wander through your wilderness, that you, too, will make it to a clearing. It may be ever so slight at first, but keep looking and someday you will be able to see the new thing that is already happening.

Help me understand so I can live.

Psalm 119:144b, *New Century Version*

I saw the angel in the marble and carved until I set him free.

Michelangelo

Look at the new thing that I am going to do.
It's already happening. Don't you see it?

Isaiah 43:19, *New Century Version*

What is hidden cannot be healed.

Sarah Ban Breathnach

♥ HEART WORK

What are your thoughts regarding childhood wounds or messages contributing to adult behaviors? What do you know about your spouse's past childhood experiences that may have been a factor in his or her devastating choices? Does your spouse have a mother wound, or a father wound? Do you have messages or wounds from your past that play a role in how you respond to your spouse? Dare to explore this area of your life so that you can find clarity and peace of mind.

If your spouse has chosen to do the work of discovering the whys of his or her betrayal and has taken full responsibility for those actions, I would suggest that you set aside time each day to process with your spouse. (If you are on your own, find a trusting friend with whom you can process appropriately.) An example might be, between 6:00 and 7:00 pm after the dinner hour, you bring to your spouse the questions or thoughts that have been nagging at you throughout the day. You may choose to read a portion of your journal if you find it difficult to get your words out. Use the "I" statements, not the "you" statements in your conversation. When the hour is up, stop, and agree to continue processing the following day. Use the rest of the discretionary time in your day to dream, to create, to read something motivational, to meet with a friend who can think forward with you and provide a positive conversation. Plan a retreat, a vacation, or work on a life plan—create a clearing for yourself.

14

TAKE HOLD OF COURAGE

You gain strength, courage and confidence
by every experience
in which you really stop to look fear in the face ...
you must do the thing you cannot do.

Eleanor Roosevelt

Journal Entry, September 25, 2004
Again and again I have confronted fear.
I crawled, I tiptoed, and at times I leaped over the
threshold of fear ...

Random Acts of Courage

What is courage? Is it an emotion, a drive, a conviction?
Perhaps it is a combination of all three. All I know is that
with each leg on my life's journey, I chose to be courageous
in the face of fear. I had to make the decision to move out
bravely into the darkness that was before me if I was to get
healthy.

The second I began this wild walk, depression and unworthiness assaulted me from all sides. I had to muster enough fearlessness to free myself from the depressing dread that threatened to overpower me. When I plummeted into the cesspools of indecision and doubt, I had to crawl inch-by-inch to freedom with positive self-talk and redirecting false messages. Entering into the dark, dank cavern of unforgiveness required more fortitude than I thought that I had. And at one juncture, I had to gain enough confidence in my Guide to believe that he knew the way out of these nightmarish woods. I learned to listen with my heart, and not to the louder, fraudulent voices. With persistence, I traversed uncertain trails, continuously on the lookout for a clearing. Somehow I knew that finding one would lead me to the end of this wilderness walk.

With great boldness I faced one adversity after another. At each juncture it was necessary for me either to face my fear with courage or to live in the pain of my fear. To choose courage would offer the hope of healing; to choose fear would offer pain without an answer. Both choices were constantly before me.

With all the choices that I made along my journey, choosing to trust again took more courage than any of the other acts that I just mentioned. Trust did not come naturally to me. I learned as a young girl not to trust anyone, or anything, not even my own intuitions. Just trying to believe that God was guiding this whole journey was difficult enough.

I had to *learn* how to trust. This took time and a certain amount of determination. Just because I decided to move out into these thorny areas did not automatically make me a trusting person. This practice of moving out and deciding to trust meant that I needed to repeat an act again and again until it became an established pattern of behavior. It took an extreme amount of courageous discipline.

Trust Again?

After Rick's disclosure of unfaithfulness, my trust button was completely disabled. I wondered if I could believe anyone ever again. I questioned everyone's motives after my husband confessed. I would look long and hard into people's faces, watching their eyes, their gestures, wondering if I would catch them in a lie. I wondered what secrets they were hiding.

I felt I had been a fool for not recognizing the red flags of betrayal that he waved in my face. My intuitions were strong, but because of my childhood messages of "don't open that door," I did not heed them. I sensed I had betrayed myself.

To trust Rick was not even an option for some time. I could not trust him for many, many months. I needed time for my wounds to heal, time to assess my losses. Eventually, I decided I was ready to trust my own heart, and one day I bravely said to Rick, "I am going to choose to trust you today." I practiced this faith-walk on a daily basis, repeating this promise. Yes, I was apprehensive; my heart had been wounded deeply. My heart had been deceived. Was it possible that it could be sliced open once more, fooled yet again? Yes, but I chose to calculate the risks, and I began weighing my options of either choosing to remain stuck in the pain, or deciding to be courageous enough to trust again. I thought this act of choosing to trust might be one of the routes that would eventually lead me out of the dark forest of betrayal.

Rick worked very hard at earning my trust. When I told him that I was choosing to trust him that day, he felt encouraged, and that gave him more confidence in his journey toward wellness. My daily promise about choosing to trust Rick spurred him on to try even harder to gain more of my trust.

> *Journal Entry, August 12, 2003*
>> *I have wondered over the last several months,*
>> *"What does trust look like, feel like?"*
>> *So, I must ask myself a few questions.*
>> *Do I believe Rick loves me?*
>> *Yes, there is no doubt in my heart, or my mind.*
>> *Do I believe he will never betray me again?*
>> *I say yes, but there is a slight cramp in my heart*
>>> *as I write this.*
>> *I know Rick understands why he did what he*
>>> *did and he would be a fool if he did this to us*
>>> *again;*
>> *I do not believe my husband is a fool.*
>> *Do I feel safe to be me? Yes.*
>> *Do I pay close attention to my intuitions? Yes.*
>> *It is much easier to say what is on my mind.*
>> *I do not feel like I am walking on eggshells*
>>> *anymore.*
>> *I am learning to trust God. I am learning to trust*
>>> *myself.*
>> *So, I must ask myself this, "Can I begin to trust Rick?"*
>> *My answer would be—yes.*

If your spouse is making the effort to prove to you every day that he or she is working toward recovery, I encourage you to dare to risk moving out into the briar bushes that have darkened your pathway. Go ahead and bravely allow your heart to be exposed to the risk of being pierced again. I know it seems costly, and you may feel that you have much to lose if you enter that place again. I know it is frightening. During this part of your journey, you may find that it is difficult (and feels downright impossible at first) to begin to trust again.

If Rick had not worked hard on his issues, if he had not pursued health and restoration and had not chosen to be selfless, then this part of our healing would have been delayed. It's possible that trust could never have been established. We both took our healing very seriously. Rick did the hard and painful work of facing his past. He began to understand the abuses of his childhood that created boundary issues and brokenness, and he did his very best to prove his love to me every day. It took both of us working persistently and willingly to make it through this complex time. We wanted to get well, no matter the cost.

Learning to trust my heart instincts took diligent work. I faced my insecurities, embraced my fears and chose to walk out onto the same frightening trails that had led me to heartache and pain. The journey would take me step-by-step toward the life that I desperately longed for in our family. It took me a very long time to learn to trust again. This process of learning to trust will require courage, just as in all the stages of this wilderness nightmare. But be brave. If your spouse is working hard at being trustworthy, take the first step out of your protected shelter and begin the journey towards trust.

New Normal

Every part of this wild walk had proven to me that, if I would choose to hold on to courage just a little while longer, and if I was willing to be vulnerable once again, I would be a little closer to finding my way out. I had to learn to be okay with the unexpected twists and turns that at first caused uncertainty.

When this "new normal" subtly ushered itself into my life, the memories of the early days still stung. The pain, the confusion, the raw emotions and the consequences of Rick's behaviors still clouded and distorted my everyday life. But, eventually the time came when our feet were standing on solid ground once again. Our new normal life began and the usual daily routines returned. Yes, there were elements of our past that were still the same. Some of Rick's behaviors that annoyed me before were still there. For instance, when he couldn't find his keys, or when he forgot to wipe down the bathroom countertop or rinse the sink after he finished with his morning shave. These minor irritations were there before his confession, but they seemed to be magnified once the violent and shaky ground of his betrayal settled down. I had to try to be diligent as I practiced patience with Rick and myself as we adjusted to the changes in our story.

One particular change that I had to adjust to was Rick showering me with words of affection and gratitude. For days and days throughout the first months of our recovery, the sentiments literally gushed from him, like a cleaned-out well or spring. This admiration and respect had never been a part of my life before; the well-guarded walls that surrounded both our hearts would not allow such emotional outpouring. I soaked up every ounce of it. I likened myself to a dried up old sponge that had been discarded under the kitchen sink and totally forgotten. Slowly I began to believe his words of affirmation and love. Trust was a huge factor here, but over the course of time my emotional sponge began to absorb his life-giving words.

During that critical time, those moments were such an important part of our healing. Once my husband confessed his infidelity, his encumbered guilt no longer had a hold on him. His secrets had weighed so heavily on his emotional wellbeing and the darkness of his shame distorted how he really felt about me. He truly did love me before the disclosure, but because of his brokenness he did not know *how* to love.

As my wounded heart began to heal and as we both worked diligently on our broken parts, I found that there was a lull or a pause in our love walk. I suddenly tripped and fell onto the road of confusion once again. This time what stopped me dead in my tracks was not unprocessed anger or fears, but rather the subtle changes that were occurring in our story.

As our daily routines once again settled into place, I would find myself longing for the deep conversations that had been a part of our early recovery. The lingering discourses were replaced with shorter, less-frequent chats. We found that we no longer fell asleep in each other arms; after a time of cuddling we would slide over to opposite sides of the bed in order to get a more restful sleep. Mundane schedules consumed the day, and the desire for

Rick to be attentive to me and my needs were fresh in my mind. I longed for those days and I mistakenly believed that this change in our relationship meant that we were experiencing lost love, that the endearing fondness that we had previously felt was gone forever. It would be a very long time before I would find that missing piece of my heart.

> *Journal Entry, December 12, 2002*
> *I feel numb most of the time.*
> *My husband loves me. God, help me feel it!*
> *Help me feel his love again.*
> *Help me feel the tingle in my heart again.*
> *I feel reserved, scared. Is this normal?*
> *I know my heart and mind are a bit messed up*
>   *right now.*
> *Help me!*

I wish that I had known that the delightful adolescent euphoria of the early days was not going to last. Those feelings of rapture, exhilaration, and ecstasy had not existed in my marriage before. I had become accustomed to Rick's gushy affections and his overly romantic admirations; I did not want those to go away. There were many times when my *own* insecurities created doubt and concern about my husband's true feelings for me. But in truth, as Rick continued to work on his broken parts and continued to heal, his love for me was growing more profoundly rich and complete. The only kind of love that we had known before had been superficial, selfish, and competitive—the kind of love in which we had to perform acts of service in order to receive anything in return. What kind of life is that? I think back on those days, and I cannot even believe that that is how we lived. Out of our brokenness we did not know how to love each other. In my life I had known only immature love, the kind of love that was contaminated from the poisoned messages of our past.

Sprains of The Heart

Even years after Rick's disclosure, there were tender areas of my heart that hurt when they were rubbed or touched. I call these painful events "sprains." These sprains, when twisted just right, ached just as sharply as they did the day of the initial injury. If you have ever sprained your ankle, you know what I am saying. Even though the swelling is gone and time has passed, it seems the muscles and tendons are vulnerable and weak. All it takes is a sudden stumble off a curb or a slip on a crack in the sidewalk, and without warning the pain of your past sprain comes charging back. The frustrating ritual follows—icing, elevating, and possibly using crutches for a few days to keep pressure off, so the ankle can heal again.

I remember one particular day when I felt the sprain of my husband's betrayal. This sprain took me by surprise; it had been some time since his confession. It was Valentine's Day, and I had tried to find a card to express my thoughts and feelings, but it was not possible. The cards were pretty enough, and they had beautiful, poetic words, but I wondered, "*How does one buy a card expressing love to the one who betrayed that love?*"

Journal Entry, February 14, 2005

Today I feel a sadness that lies beneath a veneer of love.

Today is Valentine's Day. I should be in love.

I should feel in love.

I should be excited to spend a romantic evening with my husband.

I am very thankful for the love that Rick has shown me.

I know he loves me.

But there is an ache in my heart that lingers.

I am blessed, yet I am forlorn. I am loved, and yet I am deeply alone.

I want desperately to feel the intense feelings of love that I once felt deep within my soul. I fear that it is lost forever.

My heart feels bruised today. Why did the wound appear today?

I sense deep within me that I am searching to feel something.

I am looking for lost love.

Most days, I can distract my emotions from such thoughts, but today they have risen to the surface, above the veneer and I am sad.

Love is a decision I know.

But today, I want to feel my old loving heart beat again, the way it used to feel, the way it use to love.

I am fighting tears today.

My throat swells from holding back the flow of emotion.

> *I fear if I let it loose, I will drown in my sorrows.*
> *Help me God, to find my lost love.*

Once again I was faced with the reality of my painful situation. I questioned whether I really did forgive my husband and, just as I had done so many times in the past, I embraced my pain and mourned another loss. I then decided to nurse my wounded heart back to health, choosing to move forward once again.

As the new normal took over our lives, stormy days of change would continue to rattle my world. When the dry days of loneliness and solitude crashed on my soul, it would cause me to question my husband's love for me. But what I discovered during that season was that a healthy relationship was developing. After so many years of false ideas of what I thought true love was supposed to be, I eventually chose to believe that our love was not lost, just different. I had to mourn the loss of those first feelings of adolescent affection. I learned that when the exhilarating feelings of puppy love faded, it did not mean that my husband's love for me was gone. Once again, I had to embrace the pain and mourn the loss of my innocent, juvenile infatuations and fairytale love stories.

Mature love had to come, or I would have found myself living in an unhealthy fantasy world. So, with bold belief I moved forward and accepted the new relationship that was emerging. Over time I found that Rick's love for me had not waned, but it had grown richer, deeper, and fuller than I could have ever dreamed.

Looking back now after all these years, I can recall the day when I realized that my dried, shriveled sponge had been completely filled up. I didn't have to *do* anything to get Rick to love me; it was pure, unconditional love. Rick's affections and praise still continue to this day. My sponge is still full and overflowing with the richness and completeness of his love.

Journal Entry, October 11, 2005
> *The transformation of our relationship has been remarkable.*
> *In the beginning of our recovery journey I needed Rick to adore me in the way that he did.*
> *I was desperate for love.*
> *My heart was like an old sponge, withered and completely dry.*
> *But now, I have soaked up every ounce of the love that Rick has showered on me.*
> *I am a dripping wet sponge, full of the knowledge of his love for me.*
> *Rick has shown his affections for me over and over ...*

E-mail to my brother Kevin, December 2006
> *Good morning! Thanks for the birthday greetings! I received the best birthday present in the world! I do not have to wait for my birthday to know that my husband loves me. He proves his love to me everyday of the year. Prior to our life-changing event I would only feel Rick's love, or his attempt at it on the days that the calendar says it was important to do so. When I woke up today I became very emotional knowing that I am loved everyday. That is a gift in itself!*

Dislodging Emotional Debris

If I had chosen not to trust again and not to be vulnerable to love, I would have begun the unhealthy practice of stuffing my emotional pain and memories of my husband's betrayal. Then, just like a raging river after a heavy rainstorm, the swift waters of denial would have swallowed the debris of my pain that had been collecting on the riverbanks of my life. As the churning waters tossed and the ravaging thoughts churned deep within, I may have dismissed the warning signs of unprocessed pain and anger. My mind would have repeatedly tried to bury the grief of the betrayal, but eventually my body would not have been able to withstand the pressure that was building deep inside. My body, my health would have suffered greatly. I have seen it over and over in many wounded people.

You may think that you have the power within yourself to move on without doing the difficult work of discovering the brokenness that this trauma has left. You may believe that you can't afford counseling, or that you do not have the time to invest in your recovery process. If this is the path that you choose, then I believe that one day the mental debris will unexpectedly reappear, causing damage to you and those around you.

I am sure that you have seen TV coverage after heavy rainstorms. You have witnessed all the wreckage, the fallen trees and even whole buildings that become dislodged because of flooding rivers. The storm can damage the bridges that cross these raging waters and the erosion of the banks can change a river forever. The powerful force of flash floods can knock even strong structures off of their footings; the damage done to the concrete foundations cost hundreds of thousands of dollars to repair. The reconstruction of roads and overpasses can cause people to alter their travel routes for months while the restoration work is being done.

Our lives are like this. We are not strong enough to withstand the assault of buried and denied emotional trauma. These raging emotions will find their way out. If not in any other way, the hidden fragments of our pain can and usually will create serious health concerns. High blood pressure, sleep disorders, heart disease, chronic pain, weight problems—the list of effects goes on and on.

You have to make many choices on this wilderness walk. You can choose to face courageously each fear and choose to move forward. Some things are certain. If you choose to try to reject this life that has been dealt you, if you refuse to work on your *own* brokenness, if you refuse to look inside *yourself* and do the hard work that it takes to become a healthy person, you may live the rest of your life unfulfilled, cynical and lonely. You will live that life because you will likely never allow anyone to enter into your world again, either to hurt you or to love you. Instead you must be willing to be hurt again, to trust once more and to love again. I know how frightening these choices may be for you.

The well-known author, C.S. Lewis, was a wise man; he knew a thing or two about pain, love, and life. Grasp the significance of what he is saying.

To love at all is to be vulnerable. Love anything, and your heart will certainly be wrung and possibly broken. If you want to make sure of keeping it intact, you must give your heart to no one, not even to an animal. Wrap it carefully round with hobbies and little luxuries; avoid all entanglements; lock it up safe in the casket or coffin of your selfishness. But in that casket, —safe, dark, motionless, airless—it will change. It will not be broken; it will become unbreakable, impenetrable, irredeemable.[7]

Courageous Trust

Was I going to be willing to trust again, to risk being hurt again? I had to find whatever courage I could and choose to love, even when I felt no love at all. I struggled for quite some time with this; it did not come easily. I had to resolutely resist all the voices of my past experiences and heartbreaks in order to move forward on my journey toward a restored life. It took more courage than I thought I had. No matter how difficult or painful it was, somehow I knew that, if I tried to numb my pain, it would only delay the healing.

When a woman gives birth to a child, she knows that the pain will subside, but she must push through the pain to birth a new life. I found that, as I continued to push past the pain over and over again, eventually the pain subsided and my wounded heart began to heal. Find the courage to push past this pain, my friend—push!

Journal Entry, January 11th, 2006

Three years, three months and five days since that surreal October afternoon—the day my life was altered forever.

I now ponder; yes ponder over all that has happened. I shouldn't be, but I am totally amazed—amazed at what God has done. So much life, so much healing and yet so much pain.

2005 is now over and I want it recorded that I made it through another year of recovery.

So many lessons have been learned.

Mature love has been cultivated; forgiveness has been expressed.

Trust in God is being formed; I am learning to trust my husband again.

This has been quite a challenge for me; I have had a few heart stopping moments along the way.

I have witnessed my sons grow up some this year.

I have become a better mother and I am learning to be a better wife.

I thank God for the courage to open doors that before would have caused so much fear.

I thank God for teaching me that I am worthy!

It has been difficult and at times overwhelming, but I am a stronger person because of the pain—the trials.

God has given me strength, and at times God has carried me.

*I believe that God is pleased with me; he is smiling
    at me!*
I feel freer to be me and I can laugh at myself.
My life is moving on; I am moving on!!!

*Courage is resistance to fear, mastery of
fear—not absence of fear.*

Mark Twain

*This is courage,
to bear unflinchingly what heaven sends.*

Euripedes

*I have found a paradox.
That if I love until it hurts
then there is no hurt but only more love.*

Mother Teresa

*Courage gives stamina when love is gone,
faith is wavering, and prayer difficult.*

Frances J. Roberts

♥ HEART WORK

Trust again? Is it possible after an injury such as this? Is it possible not only to trust the one who betrayed your trust, but to trust anyone ever again? Whether your marriage is intact or not, it is vital for your emotional wellbeing that you work diligently on your trust issues. This leg of your healing journey can take a long time, as it should. Just as in the forgiveness phase, you should not rush this time, nor should you reconstruct protective barriers to protect yourself, as this will only create more hardships in your future. Resist the temptation to ignore the debilitating debris that can collect in your heart and mind. Learn to trust your heart with this challenging phase and expect heart sprains to occur now and again. Courageously choose to embrace each pain and mourn each loss until a sense of renewed peace has been attained. Bravely decide to move on with each leg of your healing journey.

Continue to process your feelings in the way that you have found works best for you.

15
NEVER GIVE UP

*I have sometimes been wildly, desperately,
acutely miserable, racked with sorrow,
but through it all still know quite certainly
that just to be alive is a grand thing.*

Agatha Christie

A Voice in The Darkness

A few years have transpired since my worst nightmare came to pass and I find myself staring back into the distant wilderness valley that is now behind me. As I reflect back on my journey through the wild lands of my husband's unfaithfulness, I can vividly recall the crushing despair that stalked my mind. I remember when hopelessness consumed every part of my being. Yet, for reasons I cannot explain, one thought held me captive and kept me from literally drowning in my anguish. I clung desperately to the belief that, just maybe, life could be better than before. I somehow believed that, in order for me to survive my wilderness nightmare, I must never give up hope that there was a life waiting for me, a life that I had desired for so long.

Throughout these pages I have set out to be a voice calling back to the wounded faithful. I have shared snapshots from my life's journey through the wilderness of betrayal to encourage you, the wounded faithful, as you traverse through your own paths of devastation and despair. I have heard the cries of the lost one echoing through the canyons of disillusionment and grief. I am acquainted with the haunting question of how to move forward when everything in your life is now shattered, mangled, and torn. I am quite familiar with the mind-maddening reruns of "what if" and "now what" scenarios as I dangled on the mountainside of fear and desperation. I have intimately known the uncertainties of whether or not I could hang on while my world was crumbling all around me, when it felt as if all hope was gone.

Weary and heart-broken wanderer, please try to hear my voice as I call out to you in the darkness of your own wilderness nightmare. "Hold tight." "Hang on just a while longer." "Please do not give up; never give up!"

The Power of Hope

Stories of survival have always captivated me. As I have listened to the amazing accounts of each survivor, I noticed a common thread that binds all of them together: the ones who had hope survived. The following stories illustrate the power of such hope.

A man who had planned and prepared his whole life to climb a mountain was overcome by a sudden snowstorm.

Barely alive, he lay unconscious on the pathway to the summit. One by one, fellow mountain climbers stopped to check his vital signs. Believing that he was too far-gone, they left him for dead. Several hours passed as a brutalizing mountain blizzard battered this mountaineer. No one should have survived, but this man did.

A Holocaust victim lived through the terror and torture of a Nazi concentration camp. This survivor could have remained a prisoner of his life story as nightmares of the carnage replayed over and over in his mind. But he did not.

A young solo rock climber falls and becomes lodged by a boulder in a narrow canyon. The only way he could free himself was to cut off a portion of his arm with a small pocketknife and walk miles out of a canyon. He could only have attempted such a feat because he chose to live.

These stories of survival intrigue me. I have wondered how these individuals could survive such unbelievable pain and extreme circumstances. I believe it was because of the powerful emotional drive of hope. These inspirational people wanted a second chance; they wanted another opportunity to have their lives make sense.

Would their lives ever be the same after their ordeals? Never. But just as Emily Dickinson so beautifully wrote in one of her poems, they chose to believe that "'Hope is the thing with feathers, that perches in the soul.'"[8] With this hope they accepted their circumstances and boldly set out and made the decisions to live.

The man who survived the vicious storm on top of the mountain lives every day with deformed hands, feet and a reconstructed nose because of the damaging effects of frostbite. But he chose not to let the mountain defeat his dreams of climbing, and he will once again face the large peak that nearly took his life.

The Jewish man has lived every day of his long life with the sting of horror that he witnessed while in bondage, but he chooses to share his life story by bringing inspiration and hope to others. And the young man who cut off his own arm continues to live out his passions of climbing and hiking. Amazing!

But, you say, a loved one did not betray them. It is one thing to be savagely attacked by nature and by your enemies, but it is quite another thing to be betrayed by someone you thought you could trust—someone you loved. This is much more difficult to bear and overcome.

You are right, but if you reflect for a minute on the stories of those who struggled to survive their tragedies, you will notice that they *chose* to survive. They did struggle. You can be sure that they had many moments, hours and, for some, years of emotional torment. But they made a decision to live and, with a second chance at life, they wanted to live it to its fullest.

Do you have that kind of hope? Are you willing to struggle through your recovery and fight to push past the pain and grief that is now consuming your life? Do you want to survive this nightmare? Are you willing to be an inspiration to others—your family and friends and yes, even strangers— as you share with them your story of survival and second chances?

I encourage you to press past this time of hopelessness and despair and choose never to give up. You can live in anticipation of a life that you have always dreamed of.

Survival Methods That Instruct

With much vulnerability, chapter after chapter, I have attempted to share with you from my heart. I have shared about my brokenness and my methods of survival, some that worked, and some that did not. I have shared stories and journal entries that described how lost and frightened I was. With honest openness I told how I struggled with forgiveness and trust.

I may not have always navigated in the way that I would have preferred. I may have taken a more difficult route than my Guide would have chosen. But looking back now on my journey, I would not alter one moment or detail of my recovery. I am being truthful when I say I would never go back and live the life I had before, NEVER! Yes, the living nightmare was unbearably painful and at times emotionally debilitating, but the isolation and the emptiness that I carried with me for all those years prior to my husband's disclosure was even more so.

Some of you may be saying to yourself, *"But my life was so perfect before."* I have to ask: Was it really perfect? Really? I recently had a conversation with a woman who truly believes she had the ideal childhood, an idyllic life prior to her wedding. No childhood traumas, a real *"Leave It to Beaver"* life. She shared that she felt she had been duped when she married her husband. She believes that he wore a mask of normalcy along with his shiny armor and she had no idea he had a broken past. I do believe that it is possible for someone to fall in love with a poser; one who for many years has hidden behind a thick wall of shame, for too much was at risk. If others knew who was behind the mask and polished protective covering, no one would ever love him. It was only after

249

living in the same house, day in and day out, that the broken-ness of unprocessed wounds began to reveal the chinks in his now dull and dented armor.

Unless you have been married only a very short time, you have systems and behaviors that repeat themselves over and over, creating unresolved relational issues and dis-contentment. Even if you are one of the blessed to have had no trauma in your past, and you had a wonderful child-hood, but it was only after you said "I do" that you realized you married a stranger, you will still have work to do. In order for you to move forward it is vital to discover the whys of your responses or non-responses to issues that have invaded your life.

Lessons from A Former Victim

In my own wanderings I fell among prickly briars and I found myself stuck for quite some time as I struggled against the thorns. This instructional phase was a long and painful one for me.

I found that, after Rick confessed, I *wanted* to be the vic-tim of my husband's choices. I didn't realize that I was des-perately holding onto this role until I received a phone call from a man who had been unfaithful to his wife a few years earlier. He called to check on Rick and me, to see how our marriage restoration process was going. After a few minutes of conversation, the details of which I truly cannot remember, he asked me candidly, "Patti, do you think that you are better than your husband?" I was shocked at his question, and to be quite truthful I was pretty angry with him. I responded sharply in my mind, *"How dare you even think that or even ask that about me! I am the one who was hurt here, don't you remember that?"* I couldn't get off the phone fast enough.

But after that phone conversation, I found myself pushing the replay button over and over in my mind, as if it had been recorded. I was able to pull myself away from the noxious thorns that were penetrating my heart just long enough to realize that I had been benefiting from the role of faithful victim. After much heart reflection and honest self-talk, I had to admit that at times I *did* feel I was a better person than my husband. I felt that I was "holier than him," and I would hold this attitude high and wave it frequently in his face. This condemnation did not bring the desired results. I realized that my attitude was hindering the healing process in my marriage.

When I held myself higher than my husband, I allowed myself to become judge and juror over our circumstances. I did not have that authority over Rick. This was quite a challenge for me, but if I had allowed it to continue, I could have destroyed any chance of rebuilding my marriage.

Yes, I was a victim of my spouse's choices, but I had to decide to let go of this role. This was another process in mourning. I mourned the loss of no longer being the injured party, the hurt one, the faithful one. I needed to repeat this often; the brokenness and the anger inside of me fought against this practice and my resistance to giving up my need to be the victim was very strong.

If giving up the victim role is difficult for you as well, then you will need to ask yourself why you cling to it. Maybe this victim role has been played out in your life before. Perhaps as a child you had been abused, or neglected, or abandoned by a busy or emotionally absent parent, and you have lived your life feeling like you have been treated unfairly. Or, perhaps life has battered you in many ways and you have been bruised with self-doubt and regret— and this recent nightmarish event created a perfect storm in which you could release all the pent up pressure.

For most of my life, I saw myself as just one big mess. My existence on planet earth has been one painful ordeal after another, and I struggled constantly with thoughts of "*Okay, this makes sense to me; what's another scar on my already mangled heart. I deserve this.*" Or "*This will just make me a tougher woman.*" I felt I had no control over the outcomes of the trials that were inflicted upon me. I believed that my ability to find contentment and happiness in my life *or not* was a direct result of those events.

If I had stayed frozen in that state of denial and blame, I would never have made the significant life changes I needed to make. I realized that, when I became a victim of life's circumstances, then I relinquished my ability to make choices that could create a better life. I learned this behavior from my father. He had always been a victim. Many, many times as a child, I heard the same account of all the wrongs that had been dealt him, and even now as an adult my father will talk about his woes and make no changes to improve his life.

Once I discovered the self-pity source, then it was my responsibility to decide to make choices that improved my life. I chose to pursue the healthiest life that I could possibly have, and with that decision I chose not to see myself as a victim of my life's circumstances. That decision has changed the way I view my world. It has helped with my negative attitudes, and as an added benefit, I do not suffer from the symptoms of life-depleting depression any longer.

Yet Another Lesson—The Dance

Marriages are like a dance that only the two will share. Both know how *not* to step on each other's toes, but if we are truly honest with ourselves, we know we can easily confuse the rhythm and change the tempo of our dance by a slight facial gesture or by cutting words that can send sharp, condemning shock waves through our partners. The good old silent treatment, or the expressive partner who is always ready with a critical comment, can be just as destructive to the rhythm of our dance, and as you know, our body language speaks louder than words. We have all been guilty of one or all of these.

I benefitted greatly by my passive aggression in my marriage. One of the ways that I could quickly get out of a conflict—change the dance move—was by making one of these comments to Rick: "You are talking down to me," or "You are treating me like a child," or "You act like you are my father." These accusations would trigger a response in Rick that felt rewarding to me. My husband would tell me that he could never have an adult conversation with me because I *acted* like a child, then he would storm out of the room and the conflict was over, at least for a time. This survivor response worked for me.

These "side steps" would shut down my husband faster than anything else that I could have done. Now, you must understand, until I did some very difficult work on my own issues, I did not even know that this was a maneuver I subconsciously used to shift the dance. I discovered how I could masterfully say just the right combination of words that would satisfy my need to hurt Rick, and I derived comfort knowing I had hurt him. I finally realized how manipulative these statements were and how harmful and destructive they were to our relationship.

This was just one of the many factors that contributed to our unhealthy marriage. Our conflicting dance moves prevented us from ever having the intimacy with each other that we both so desperately wanted. As the years went by and both of us danced and stumbled and tripped our way across the floor of our married life, we created an environment of silent chaos, with a few outbursts of cutting words and body gestures that landed us in desperate times.

As couples, no matter how many years you have been together, you have learned to sweep across the dance floor of your life together with caution, aggression, and passion. However, if you find yourselves tripping up, or when you become uncomfortable with the moves, or you are bored with the same old mundane steps, you must look at the deeper issues.

You did not cause your spouse to have an affair—this was his or her own choice. However, every marriage has seasons when relational disrepair develops, hindering a couple's ability to maintain true intimacy. Sexual infidelity was a warning, like a dance instructor's whistle screeching to get you to stop twirling on the dance floor and pay attention to his instruction. It pierced your heart and soul as your life, your dance, suddenly came to a crashing halt. You were both out of step, and as a result, your dance has been changed forever—as have the dance partners.

If you choose not to do the hard work of discovering your own brokenness, you will not learn how you can heal from the wounds of betrayal. Your trust issues will forever go unhealed, unchanged. And then, time moves forward and eventually you *will* dance again. You will twirl, bend and dip just as you did before. The dance may look a little different, it may be to a different tune, and you might even have a different partner. But one thing is certain; your healing will be incomplete. You will not be capable of trusting your partner not to step on your toes or drop you on the floor. Your heart will be numb and your life may never be fulfilled.

In contrast, if you decide not to give up and are willing to do the difficult work, your new dance moves will cause everyone on the ballroom floor of your life to stop and take notice. You've seen this in the movies or on television, couples gracefully, quietly gliding across the floor with mesmerizing moves that stop the crowd of dancers. Everyone steps back to make room for the couple and watch in respectful awe and wonder. There is no stepping on toes, just smooth graceful dips and bends or fast jitterbug twists and jigs.

I believe that this nightmare that has robbed you of your dreams can in fact become the turning point, enabling you to dance the dance that you have so long sought after, with the partner you have always dreamed of.

Hope Rising

With each one of the steps that you take toward health, you are building a strong structure of hope. As you face your emotional injury (whether it is this recent heartbreak or your childhood wounds), as you address each issue, you will begin placing one stepping-stone of confidence on top of another. You will begin to feel your hope rising. The mounting self-assurance will continue to grow as you pursue hope and wellness. This is difficult and draining work.

You cannot rebuild your life without laboring emotionally, physically, and spiritually.

Do not give up! Work hard at discovering your broken parts. They are there. Choose to believe that you can truly have the life that is waiting for you beyond the devastating rubble that surrounds your heart right now. Never give up on the hope, and then one day you will look back and know that your grief and anguish were not in vain.

I believe that, if I had not pursued emotional health, I would not have been capable of withstanding the onslaught of anguish that my nightmare produced. Believe me, there were times when I thought I might collapse under the weight of the pain of Rick's unfaithfulness. There were many days and nights on this wilderness journey when I was numb to my circumstances. I often felt I must be the most unlovable person on this planet. I had to will myself to believe that God loved me, and in the process of all of my new discoveries, I eventually began to love myself.

I learned many lessons on this journey. I learned that I could not make it on my own. If I had not cried out to God for help, I am not certain I would have survived my wilderness journey and learned healthy ways of recovering. Over time, my trust in God began to grow, even though I hesitated and faltered in my efforts. I discovered that God understood my disbelief, and I chose to believe that He would never abandon me. With never-ending patience my Guide would wait for me until I gathered enough courage to move out into the darkness that lay before me.

As I have shared my journey of how I survived my worst nightmare, I pray that you have decided that you, too, can and will survive yours. I hope that you will find the courage to face your pain, that you will practice embracing each excruciating loss. I hope you will learn to mourn those losses, so you can begin to move forward on your journey toward restoring your life. My desire, as you have joined me in this story of my journey, is that you have begun the long and difficult process of thinking about forgiveness. And, as you have listened with your heart, I pray that you will decide that you are ready—ready to trust in your Guide, to trust in yourself, and, if your spouse has proven that they are trustworthy, ready to trust in them once again.

My faithful friend, as you continue your wilderness walk, cling to hope. Hang on tightly to God's guiding hand. Don't let go. I encourage you to continue to be courageous and peer deeply into the dark, scary paths that are before you. Begin creating a new life for yourself, not for your spouse, not for your children, but for you. Never give up hope that you can have the life that you desire. It can become a reality. Never give up, my friend.

I set out on this journey to come alongside you, to encourage you and to let you know that you are not alone. My hope is that my story has helped you begin the healing that your heart cries out for. I hope that you continue your search for True North, which signifies your own awakening from the nightmarish hell that shattered your dreams. I am hopeful that one day I will have the privilege of seeing you on the ballroom floor of your life, dancing and twirling as you have never danced before.

*Hope is faith
holding out its hand in the dark.*

George Iles

*God, my God, I yelled for help and you put me together.
God, you pulled me out of the grave, gave me another
chance at life.*

Psalm 30:2-3, *The Message*

*We have troubles all around us, but we are not defeated.
We do not know what to do, but we do not give up the
hope of living.*

II Corinthians 4:8, *New Century Version*

*So God has given both his promise and his oath.
These two things are unchangeable because it is
impossible for God to lie.
Therefore, we who have fled to him for refuge
can have great confidence as we hold to the
hope that lies before us.*

Hebrews 6:18, *New Living Translation*

I waited and waited and waited for God.
At last he looked; finally he listened.
He lifted me out of the ditch, pulled me from the deep mud.
He stood me up on a solid rock to make sure
I wouldn't slip.
He taught me how to sing the latest God-song,
a praise song to our God.
More and more people are seeing this:
they enter the mystery,
abandoning themselves to God.

Psalm 40:1-3, The Message

❤ HEART WORK

Many times throughout my journey I became weary from all the life lessons—they seemed unending. In frustration I would scream out at God, "When can I graduate from this school?!!" Until I got my passing grade, I had to will myself to press on. How do you feel about the school that you are in right now? What are you learning about yourself? What impact are your own life lessons making on you personally?

Do you find that you are struggling with being a victim of your spouse's choices? If so, can you trace back to where this may have begun? Are you willing to face, embrace, mourn and let go of this role?

Think about your marital dance. What did you do (consciously or unconsciously) to confuse the rhythm or change the tempo of your dance? What "side-steps" were used by you and your spouse to either avoid conflict or to maintain control in your relationship?

I shared how I refused to give up on the belief that my life could be better than it was before my nightmare shattered my dreams. Do you have that kind of hope? If so, describe in detail what that life looks like for you. This will be a wonderful reference point to go back to later on in your journey. If you do not have that hope, journal with detail what you would like your life to look like. Make a checklist and work on one life goal at a time. Examples might be: a change in your career, going back to school, or learning a new hobby or skill. Perhaps you could plan and take that dream trip you've always talked about. If this is a struggle for you, it may be important to go back and revisit the victim role tendencies. Be sure to bring this up at your next counseling session.

Hope is possible, when you *decide to believe* that what you are hoping for is possible.

Part III

The Awakening

The eyes of my eyes are opened.

E.E. Cummings

16
NORTH

You are sent into the Wilderness for one reason, and one reason only: ... find thyself.

Sarah Ban Breathnach

Wake Up! Wake Up!

Something was stirring deep within. The "eyes of my eyes" were beginning to open. Subconscious thoughts were rousing. Were my senses deceiving my weary mind? Could it be? Was I beginning to awaken from my long, tormented slumber? Was True North at last within my reach?

You have followed my footprints as I trudged along the seemingly unending trail through the wilderness of my husband's betrayal. You have read through the accounts and methods that I used to process my heart's injuries. The journey has been a long one. I often wondered how many more rugged and twisted trails I would have to tread before I awakened from this nightmare that invaded my dreams. When would my healing be complete?

Throughout the entire journey I continued to work my plan of facing, embracing, mourning and moving on. This practice empowered me to eventually find forgiveness and the courage to trust Rick once again. With the help of my Guide, I crossed over the vast valley that had stretched out before me. At long last I arrived on the other side of the wilderness. I know that the newly discovered parts of me are honest and authentic, and the character traits that are worn but polished are a direct result of my time in the wilderness.

However, upon my arrival I felt as if there was something missing. Emptiness still existed deep within my heart. I was not certain if I could ever love the way I used to love. Is love possible after an injury such as this? It seemed that, in order for me to finish this quest and write my final words for this survival guide, I had to endure yet another difficult challenge on this continuous journey.

Is Time Truly A Healer?

The old adage says, "time heals," but does it really? Does time truly heal heart wounds? I tend to believe that painful memories will slowly begin to recede amidst the normal, busy routines of life. In the end, memories do fade, leaving only tiny fragments that confirm reality.

I know there are some things on this wilderness walk that I will eventually forget. I do believe that time can create distance from our heart injuries, but God is the ultimate keeper of time. I believe that God, if allowed, is the true healer.

Journal Entry, October 6, 2007

> *As I was putting on my makeup this morning,*
> *I had to stop and think, "Has it been 4 years, or*
> *5 years?"*
> *I smiled at myself as I stared into the mirror.*
> *I have worked hard on my past brokenness,*
> *and I have successfully torn down my strong,*
> *emotional walls.*
> *I am thankful for a husband who has proven*
> *his love and commitment to me over and over.*
> *I am thankful as well for his ability to understand*
> *that trust has to be earned.*
> *We have worked very hard, and we are both*
> *healing ...*
> *As I reflect back over the last few years I am*
> *choosing to believe that the keeper of time is*
> *the one who healed my broken heart.*

With tender guidance, God introduced me to the life I had so long desired. Rick has become a better man because of our story; because of the pain of the journey, Rick has a humble spirit and a gentleness that did not exist before. My husband has a capacity to love that is beyond my earthly dreams. I feel honored that my decision to survive, to be courageous in the face of fear, was an important piece in changing the course for the future of our family.

Frances Roberts said profoundly, "The past you cannot change, but today is yours. Live it to the fullest of your awakening awareness. Don't miss an opportunity to turn every moment 'inside out'...to reveal the hidden glory, the potential with which God has invested it."[9]

When I read that statement I pictured the backside of a tapestry hanging on a museum wall. Hidden behind the intricate embroidered artwork is a knotted, tangled mess. When the backside is exposed, all the disheveled yarn and fiber denotes the difficult process that went into creating such a remarkable masterpiece.

As a result of my journey through the wilderness, I can now say that I *am* living a new life. Yes, I do have memories that I wish were not a part of me, but I believe those painful experiences add to the richness and color of the tapestry of my life. In the end they, too, will fade and blend beautifully into the handiwork of God. It took some time, but I did learn to embrace the many colors of character that transformed my world as I continued my search for True North. I can now say that the pain of my past was not wasted; I *am* living my life inside out!

Blind Trust

The summer of 2008 would become the most difficult time of my life, second only to my husband's disclosure. After four years we felt that our healing and restoration was complete and we were being led by God to move from Washington back to Idaho to start a new church. This decision to leave our boys, our new daughter-in-law, future grandbabies, our church family and our wonderful home would leave me mourning like I had not done in years. I wondered if we were doing the right thing to leave all we loved to move back to the place of my nightmare. We were to return to the familiar sights and people, to revisit the emotions from which I just spent the last six years trying to heal, the very emotions and places that had torn my heart into shreds. Was I ready for this? God's leading was very strong, and with blind trust, accompanied by the heat of summer, we packed up our belongings and moved away from all that we loved.

Our arrival back to Idaho was a bit overwhelming. Starting a new church was much more difficult than it had been when we were younger. We found that, with the demands and stress of getting this new venture up and running, we tired more easily. Plus, to complicate it further, Rick got pneumonia the day he and the U-Haul arrived. It took a few weeks for Rick to recover.

Autumn arrived and quickly passed. The last of the crispy, brown leaves clung desperately to the nearly bare trees, signaling that winter was on its way. However, it was not the chill of the approaching season that we dreaded. Another vicious storm was brewing, numbing our senses with shock and concern. This cruel tempest would create a new kind of fear, one that we had never known before. God's hand had directed us back to Idaho, away from family and friends. Why would He do such a thing during a time like this?

The decision to move back to Idaho would be just one more step forward in finding complete healing from a nightmare that assaulted my dreams so many years before. My survival journey was almost complete. If I would be patient, I would see and understand. With the recent move we had to re-establish new physicians and marker tests were done that would not have been necessary if we had we stayed in Washington. Rick's diagnosis of cancer would now be a part of our story. As the fury of this new vicious storm battered our lives, the winds of fear and confusion brought with it something that I thought I had lost forever.

> *Journal Entry, December 30, 2008, 1:30 AM*
>> *I just arrived home from a day that was like no other.*
>> *Today I faced death, and in mockery and jest it stared right back at me.*
>> *In a moment, without warning, fleeting memories rushed through my mind of days long ago.*
>> *Do I really love him?*
>> *Have I really forgiven him?*
>> *Does my heart deceive me?*
>> *As I listened to the chaotic chimes and alarms ringing simultaneously my heart and mind were in a race.*
>> *Frantic emotions ran wild. Confusion everywhere.*
>> *Large pools of tears flowed from my heart, as well as my eyes.*
>> *Rick's breathing was so laborious, so difficult.*
>> *Would this be the last sound I would hear from him, gasping for breath?*
>> *I was told to coach my husband.*
>> *With fear and trembling, I summoned a calm voice,*
>> *"Breathe Rick, breathe. Take another breath now.*
>> *That is good—deeper now—great job."*
>> *Over and over I coached.*
>> *Wiping the tears as fast as they flowed, I asked,*
>> *Is this how it ends?" This can't be; I will not accept this."*

It was not time. I was not going to lose my husband!

Not like this! It was not our time to say good-bye!

The long lost ache, the love that I have so long desired flooded my soul, my heart, my whole being.

During this unwelcomed time of fear and dread my lost love returned with a vengeance.

I love my husband; I am so in love with him.

I do not want to live the rest of my life without this man.

Two blood transfusions and one day in the Critical Care Unit and my husband will live!

Rick survived the trauma and complications of cancer surgery.

So here I sit, almost 24 hours since I awoke to this day like no other.

Alone and contemplating what has just transpired and relieved that the worst is over. My husband's prostate is gone, and with it the cancer that could have stolen his life.

We get another chance at life.

A new day, a new day to love, a new kind of love!

As I wipe the tears away with the back of my hand, I ponder.

How is it, in times such as these—times of chaos and fear—that a lost love can be found? That a heart, a mind, can be restored?

Yes, I ponder and now I will lay my weary body down and fall asleep with the confidence that I will awaken to a new day.

My lost love is found!

True North at last! In order for my journey to be complete, my lost love had to be found. The beast that had invaded my dreams so long ago altered my life forever. But, in spite of that brutal assault, my life was not destroyed. My journey through the wilderness of betrayal proved to be life changing. I did survive my worst nightmare and now I am fully awake. I am fully alive. The wounds of my heart have stopped bleeding.

… I could not comprehend what was happening to my life. I looked down at the devastating wound that covered the left side of my chest, and put my right hand on the deep gash, thinking that I might stop the gushing blood. I thought my life was over. As the second claw was raised to strike and give the final blow, this merciless evil creature spoke in the most terrorizing voice, "I AM GOING TO DESTROY YOUR LIFE!" As the claw came crashing down, incredible strength and power came over me. It was as if I had some supernatural force that took over all functions of my body and I was determined to fight, and even more determined to live. I was not ready to die; I would fight with everything I had in me. I grabbed its grotesque paws with both of my hands and screamed at the top of my lungs with such rage, such passion, "NO, YOU WON'T!" and shoved the beast away.

I will never forget the look in its eyes, as this hideous creature stood there confounded. The fiery contempt that had been in his eyes just seconds before was now gone. He had been defeated; confused, he turned swiftly and fled …

You kept track of my every toss and turn
through the sleepless nights,
each tear entered into your ledger,
each ache written in your book.
If my enemies run away, turn tail when I yell at them
then I'll know that God is on my side.
I'm proud to praise God, proud to praise God.
Fearless now, I trust in God ...
God, you did everything that you promised,
and I'm thanking you with all of my heart.
You pulled me from the brink of death,
my feet from the cliff-edge of doom.
Now I stroll at leisure with God in the sunlit fields of life.

Psalm 56:8-13, The Message

Never think that God's delays are God's denials.
Hold on. Hold Fast. Hold out. Patience is genius.

Georges-Louis Leclerc de Buffon

God will set things right again.

Job 33:26, New Century Version

♥ HEART WORK

One day, you too will have a survival story. You will awaken from this nightmare that has robbed you of your dreams. Your wounded heart will stop bleeding; your lost love will be found. You will be fully awake, and you will be fully alive!

Choose to believe, my faithful friend; choose to believe!

*Faith is believing what we do not see,
and the reward for this kind of faith is to see what we believe.*

Saint Augustine

A Special Thank You

Where do I begin? So many people have journeyed with me since I began this writing assignment. I will do my best to communicate my feelings regarding those who contributed to the making of this book.

First, I must thank the most important one of all, my Guide. If not for my Guide, this book would not exist. My Guide gently nudged me to share my story, so others may know that it truly is possible to survive nightmares of the heart. My Guide was patient with me, even when I doubted and asked, "Do I really need to write this down for the world to read? Really?" My Guide directed every single step along the twisted path. Through every event, every survival lesson, every courageous act, God was there, leading the way. The following people were an important part of my journey. God also led them; each one was brought into my life for a specific reason.

My forever friends, Deana and Missy, I will never forget what you did for me. Your love, your counsel, and your encouragement during the darkest of all days sustained me. Thank you.

Many women prayed for me as I diligently labored to get my story into print: Natalie, Marcy, Debra, Cami, Heather, Patti, Jolene, Carol and Karolyn. Many times, because of the emotional strain, I wanted to give up. If not for your prayers, I might have. Thank you for your prayer support.

Dave Browning, I will never forget your part in our recovery story. Thank you for your gift of second chances.

Kathlyn Mickel, thank you for mentoring me as I began this writing adventure. Your guidance helped me gather the much-needed confidence to put words to my story.

Dr. Donald Joy, what a gift you are to me! Your willingness to pour hours and hours into this project will forever be appreciated. With wisdom and patience, you advised me, from the rough first draft to the first complete edit. Thank you for all that you did to make this book what it is today. I have great respect and gratitude for you. You inspire me.

Judy Hudson, in my darkest hour your words of wisdom guided me. You counseled me to listen to my heart; I listened and I heard. Thank you.

Maggie Strowd, you were the one constant that kept me sane during the most tumultuous days of my life. You were there when I needed guidance, support and encouragement. Thank you for giving me honest counsel, even when it was difficult to hear. You have been one of my biggest cheerleaders, and I am honored to call you my friend.

Connie Browning, your last minute edits were a lifesaver for me. Thank you for taking on this project and sharing your editing gifts to help make this book a reality. Thank you, so very much, for the sacrificial giving of your time.

Months morphed into years as I worked to get this writing assignment ready to be published. I want to thank you, Rick, for your willingness to put up with my sitting hour after hour in front of the computer. I do not believe many men would be as supportive, especially if their shameful story of betrayal was being told. You never complained. I will always be grateful for what you did for me during that time. You cooked dinners and delivered them to my desk. You encouraged me to take breaks, to rest my weary mind and sore neck muscles. You never gave up on me, even when I wanted to give up on myself.

As I have often said to you, I will be forever thankful that you did not go to the grave with your secret. I *am* thankful. Even though what we went through was the most painful event of our lives, we made it, with our marriage intact, stronger than ever! Thank you for being honest, and for earning my trust once again.

APPENDIX

A Prayer for the Broken Hearted
Feelings List
Finding a Counselor
Further Reading and Resources to Assist in Your Healing
Notes
About the Author

A Prayer For The Broken Hearted

God,
I pray for the reader of these pages.
I pray for them as they stumble and crawl
through the barren wasteland of their betrayal story.

During the seasons of despair and aloneness
I pray they would gather as much courage
as they can to put their trust in you.

God, as the wounded grope their way
on unfamiliar paths of betrayal and as their battered hearts
scream blame and insults at you,
thank you for understanding.

And God, during the darkest of nights
when fear and doubt pursue their troubled minds
please comfort them.

Thank you for hearing the cries of a wounded heart.

Amen

FEELINGS LIST

HAPPY	ANGRY	SAD	AFRAID
Certain	Furious	Miserable	Helpless
Hopeful	Disgusted	Crushed	Panicky
Happy	Hurt	Humiliated	Alarmed
Excited	Bitter	Lonely	Horrified
Proud	Cheated	Lost	Intimidated
Thrilled	Distraught	Embarrassed	Petrified
Content	Indignant	Rejected	Terrified
Exhilarated	Irate	Empty	Distraught
Energetic	Livid	Ashamed	Inadequate
Overjoyed	Used	Hopeless	Anxious
Secure	Fed up	Disillusioned	Suspicious
Lucky	Aggravated	Left out	Frightened
Good	Annoyed	Down	Afraid
Special	Provoked	Hollow	Harassed
Flattered	Irked	Guilty	Uptight
Impressed	Distressed	Beaten	Worried
Eager	Turned off	Unhappy	Tense
Relieved	Irritated	Sorry	Rattled
Optimistic	Peeved	Grieved	Confused
Relaxed	Disturbed	Moody	Flustered
Delighted	Displeased	Low	Jumpy
Encouraged	Upset	Glum	Uneasy
Comfortable	Exasperated	Downcast	Jittery
Refreshed	Uptight	Blue	On edge
Satisfied	Bothered	Disheartened	Out of place
Marvelous	Put out	Apathetic	Shaky
Calm	Ticked	Sober	Nervous
Grateful	Bothered	Disappointed	Apprehensive

Finding The Right Counselor

Thousands of therapists are ready to take on new clients, but only a few are truly qualified to help with the unique issues that relate to infidelity. A recent poll revealed that 57% of couples seeking help after a spouse's affair stated that their therapy sessions were not helpful, and 23% felt their counselor was somewhat helpful, but not to the degree that they would have liked. Only 20% of the couples said they had been greatly helped by their counselor.[10] Research shows that couples in counseling have a higher percentage of a successful recovery when the affair is thoroughly explored. Couples who do not seek professional therapy after the disclosure have a much more difficult time processing the issues that plague their relationship and sadly, 80% of those who divorce after an affair later regret making that decision.

Below are four questions to ask a potential counselor.

1- Will you deal directly with the issue of the affair?

If the therapist focuses *only* on your prior marital problems, refuses to address family of origin issues, or believes the "past is just the past" and will only address moving forward into the future—say thank you for your time, and excuse yourself.

2- How will you encourage honest and open communication between my spouse and me?

If there was just one factor that could save a marriage from the devastation that an affair creates, it would be honest and skillful communication. Your counselor should expect your spouse to take full responsibility for his/her choices. No blaming and no excuses. Your counselor should encourage your spouse to tell the whole truth regarding the affair. No secrets, no withholding. The counselor should offer communication tools as a part of the recovery process.

3- How long do you believe I should be able to ask about the details of my spouse's affair?

It is normal to seek answers for many, many months after the disclosure of an affair. The length of time will not be the same for everyone; it could be more, or less, depending on the level of honest communication between you and your spouse. Your counselor should encourage you to ask your spouse questions regarding his/her unfaithfulness. (An important note: only ask a question if you are certain that you want to know the answer. When in doubt, your counselor will be able to advise you.) Your counselor should encourage your spouse to answer honestly and repeatedly, until your need to ask subsides. When you are able to talk about the details of the affair and it does not unearth extreme emotional pain that is a good indicator that you are healing and moving on.

4- Do you believe that I/we can heal from this heart wound?

Their answer should be, "Yes, to the degree that you are willing to do the hard emotional work—together and/or separately."

Do not confuse a scar with an open wound. A heart wound can heal, but the scar will always be there, though fading over time. This wound can only heal when the proper restorative process has taken place. Just like all physical wounds, the initial injury is quite painful and will possibly bleed for a short time. But, the body does what it must do to aid the healing process. The wound will be tender when touched and a scab will eventually form. The wound will be swollen and continue to be tender until the scab shrinks and slowly dissolves, leaving a scar.

Our heart wounds are the just like this. It will be critical that your counselor has the skills to help you with this long and difficult process. It is crucial that you are willing to do the heart work, so your wounds can heal in the healthiest way.

For additional help in your search, I asked Maggie Strowd, LCPC, LMFT, a Marriage and Family Counselor what you should look for in a therapist. Her response:

> "I firmly believe a counselor should have training in sexual addiction, PTSD (Post Traumatic Stress Disorder) and trauma resolution. They must have a thorough understanding of shame-based behaviors and how they manifest themselves in affairs. A counselor must be able to bring unconditional positive

regard, genuineness, warmth and empathy to any session with the person who had the affair. Otherwise he or she will feel judged and plunge back into the well of shame and betrayal. A counselor should be aware of the multiple layers in which this betrayal trauma affects the wounded spouse."

When you choose a counselor it will be important for you to feel the right chemistry—a sense of connection. It can take a significant amount of time and financial commitment to find the right therapist, but I encourage you not to give up. You are worth it!

Further Reading And Resources

Infidelity

~ *After the Affair: Healing the Pain and Rebuilding Trust When a Partner Has Been Unfaithful*

by Janis Abrahms Spring Ph.D.

~ *Torn Asunder: Recovering From an Extramarital Affair*

by David Carder

Understanding Sexual Addiction

~ *Don't Call It Love: Recovery From Sexual Addiction*

by Patrick Carnes

~ *Out of the Shadows: Understanding Sexual Addiction*

by Patrick Carnes

Healing Childhood Wounds

~ *Broken Children, Grown-Up Pain: Understanding the Effects of Your Wounded Past*

by Paul Hegstrom

~ *Healing the Shame that Binds You*
   by John Bradshaw

~ *Homecoming: Reclaiming and Championing Your Inner Child*
   by John Bradshaw

Inspirational Reading

~ *Streams in the Desert*
   by L. B. Cowman

~ *Simple Abundance: A Daybook of Comfort And Joy*
   by Sarah Ban Breathnach

~ *The Message: (The Bible in Contemporary Language)*
   by Eugene H. Peterson

Optional Reading

~ *Bold Love*
   by Dan B Allender Ph.D. and Dr. Tremper Longman
   (Forgiveness)

~ *Love Me Never Leave Me: Discovering the Inseparable Bond
   That Our Hearts Crave*
   by Marilyn Meberg (Abandonment Issues)

~ *Re-bonding: Preventing and Restoring Damaged Relationships*
   by Donald M. Joy Ph. D.

~ *The Shack*
   by William P. Young

Online Resources

http://www.surviving-infidelity-kit.com/freearticles.htm#16

http://www.healthyplace.com/support/81/groups/viewbulletin/?bulletinid=74

http://www.cdc.gov/ace/prevalence.htm (Prevalence of Individual Adverse Childhood Experiences, CDC Statistics)

http://www.cdc.gov/ace/findings.htm (CDC: Major Findings)

http://www.acestudy.org/files/AR-V1N4.pdf (More CDC information on Adverse Childhood Experiences)

http://www.youtube.com/watch?v=ICsxMjEkeak (Explore Dr. Hegstroms 14 videos)

http://www.saahelp.com/Recovery/Inner%20Child.htm

http://www.creativegrowth.com/referral.htm (John Bradshaw Center, therapist list)

http://www.brenebrown.com/welcome (Shame Study-Recommended book written by Brené Brown)

Notes

Chapter 1, Page 8-9

1 Copyright © 1996 by Janis Abrahms Spring, Ph.D. Reprinted by permission of HarperCollins Publishers

Part II, Page 109

2 Hall Laurie, An Affair of the Mind (Wheaton Ill.: Tyndale House, 1996), p.23. Used by permission of Tyndale House

Chapter 9, Page 146

3 Taken from (Streams In the Desert) by (L. B. Cowman). Copyright © 1996) by (Zondervan Publishing House). Used by permission of Zondervan, www.zondervan.com.

Chapter 12, Page 186

4 Bold Love, Dr. Dan B. Allender, Copyright 1992, Used by Permission of NavPress, All Rights Reserved. www.navpress.com (1-800-366-7788).

Chapter 13, Page 219

5 http://abcnews.go.com/Business/marital-affairs-cheating/story?id=11395926

Chapter 13, Page 219
6 http://abcnews.go.com/Business/marital-affairs-cheating/
story?id=1139592

Chapter 14, Page 239
7 Excerpt from "Charity" from THE FOUR LOVES, Copyright
© C.S, Lewis, 1960, renewed 1988 by Arthur Owen Barfield,
reprinted by permission of Houghton Mifflin Harcourt
Publishing Company.

Chapter 15, Page 247
8 Emily Dickinson (1830–86) Complete Poems Part One
(Boston: Little, Brown, and Company, 1924), Used by permission of Little, Brown and Company.

Chapter 16, Page 268
9 Francis J. Roberts, Progress of Another Pilgrim (Ohio, Barbour
Publishing, 1970), p. 24

Finding the Right Counselor, Page 283
10 Overview of Report of Survey on Extramarital Affairs by
Peggy Vaughan

About The Author

Patti enjoys traveling, camping in the wild,
reading historical novels and designing garden rooms.
She loves her family, her overly affectionate
Golden Retriever, long conversation and strong coffee.
Patti is passionate about helping the betrayed learn how to
survive their nightmare stories.

Surviving Your Worst Nightmare:
A Guide For The Betrayed
is a result of that passion.

surivingyourworstnightmare.com

Made in the USA
Lexington, KY
17 July 2011